MW01640287

Born Under a Lucky Star

Born Under a Lucky Star

Anecdotes from the Life of

David C. Hawley

(Front cover) David Hawley's personality shines through in this photograph from the November 3, 1945, *Saturday Evening Post*. The article gave a humorous look at his experiences in the South Pacific.

Printed in the United States

ISBN 978-1-58597-437-5
Library of Congress Control Number: 2007932367

4500 College Boulevard
Overland Park, Kansas 66211
888-888-7696
www.leatherspublishing.com

ABOUT DAVID HAWLEY

David C. Hawley was born May 19, 1919 in Detroit, Michigan but spent most of his life in Kansas City, Missouri. He was a wonderful storyteller, and at an early age determined he would write a book about his life.

His life was, in fact, a series of adventures worthy of storytelling.

He was one of those characters with many aspects to his personality. He was intelligent and resourceful. He was a risk-taker, but when he made a leap of faith he still landed on his feet. David was charismatic and could talk his way out of any difficult situation. Physically, he was not a big man but what David lacked in stature, he made up for in charm.

In his youth he often stretched the patience of his parents and teachers. As a young man he loved to have a good time and his goal in life seemed to be to try to have as much fun as possible. As a Navy volunteer in World War II he experienced many "snafus" but still managed to come away unscathed. Even he admitted he was "born under a lucky star that never goes behind a cloud." As he matured into adulthood, he proved to be a hard worker, a good father and a hero.

From his high school experiences in the Depression, through marriage and family life, David Hawley lived to the fullest and perceived the world around him with great humor and insight. Whether you knew David Hawley or not, you will find his life story fascinating. He was quite a guy!

His memoirs covered only 1934 through 1961 but tell a lifetime of tales. The stories have been edited for brevity: he often tried "to make a long story short..." but had trouble doing so.

Ann Vernon, editor

TABLE OF CONTENTS

CHAPTER 1
THE HIGH SCHOOL YEARS

Southwest High School

Early in my Junior year in high school, at age 15, I got my first tuxedo. The tux had been given to Jimmy Campbell by a wealthy aunt in New York. Jimmy had never worn it. I bought it from him for five dollars and took it to the Jewish tailor at Sixty-Third Street to have it altered to fit me. The tailor pointed out to me that the tuxedo came from Best and Company in New York and deserved a good job.

In my parents' bedroom there was a full-length mirror. When I put that tux on with the starched collar and the bow tie, I felt like I looked like a million dollars. I couldn't wait for the Christmas dances to start.

The year was 1934, and the whole country was in a terrible depression. It was one of the worst years for Kansas City. My father's business had run out of money, and he had closed his office and moved his desk into what had been the maid's room at home. It wasn't easy for him to get the space. When he told

Peggy Pimlot, the maid, that she would have to leave because he couldn't pay her any longer, she said she couldn't leave because she had no place to go. She said she would stay and work for nothing, and for a while, she did. She eventually got a job at the Armour Packing House working on the dog food line and later married the Railway Express delivery man.

I had plenty of opportunity to wear my new tuxedo. For the lucky few there was a very active social life at our high school: there were six or eight fraternities and an equal number of sororities. Each one gave a Christmas party complete with dinner and orchestra. It was the day of the big bands. The girls wore long dresses and the boys wore tuxedos if they had one. If you had a date, you bought her a corsage. Most corsages were made from gardenias, but if you went first class, you bought her an orchid.

The dances were held at a country club or a downtown hotel. Most of those teenage kids in those expensive clothes, eating that expensive dinner and dancing to that expensive music, came from homes where their parents couldn't pay their bills. In some cases, that included their mortgage payments. Each of those dances required an invitation, but I was extremely fortunate. I had an older sister in a sorority who had enough clout to get me included in the inner circle. My other asset was that I loved to dance. The more I danced, the better that tuxedo looked.

Life During the Depression

My mother never really accepted the Depression. One evening, shortly after my father closed his office and brought his desk home, he arrived home to find a crew of men painting our house. My father couldn't believe it, and when he complained to my mother, she replied that he had seemed so depressed the last couple nights she thought she would do something that would cheer him up. She said a man who is down should come home to a bright, cheery house. She continued this line of thinking until the piano caper.

We had an old, satisfactory upright piano. My mother played it haltingly, and my sister, Harriett, took lessons on it. At the worst time in the financial history of the Hawleys, my mother used the upright as a down payment on a new baby grand piano. When Dad came home and saw it, he hit the roof. When he said he was going to send it back, my mother said he couldn't because she had already shown it to all the neighbors. Dad said if they had watched it arrive, they could watch it leave. He called Jenkins Music Company, and the next day they came and got it. Mother felt like all the neighbors watched the piano leave. We never got the upright back.

Dad's money outlasted many of the neighbors'. Our house was almost paid for when the hard times came, and he got a new mortgage on it. The day finally came that he couldn't make the mortgage payment, but the insurance company had foreclosed so many houses on our block they didn't want any more. They begged him to keep the house and pay them anything he could. President Roosevelt's Home Owners Loan Corporation saved the day. They made Dad a new loan so he could pay off the insurance company. When he got so he couldn't make the loan payment, their representative came to call. They made a new loan and lowered the payments. When Dad couldn't make this payment, the man came back and made a new loan with lower payments. I asked Dad how long it would take to pay the loan off, and he said he didn't know, but neither of us would live that long.

Through it all, my sister Harriett and I kept dancing. The biggest change in our home life was that Dad did the dishes instead of Peggy Pimlot. This was wonderful for us kids, because he recited poetry all through the dishes. If you wanted to listen to the poetry, you had to get a towel and dry. His favorites were Kipling and Service, but he had many, many more. When he recited one of Kipling's poems about India, I felt like I was there. And when he was on a Robert W. Service kick, I could feel the freezing winds of the Yukon blowing through my parka.

1934 was a wonderful year for me. I enjoyed school. I loved the social life, and I was in love with one girl after another. I wasn't old enough to drive, so I double-dated with one of my fraternity brothers. A lot of the time, I went with Tom Bierly. Tom was a year older, and his father, who had lost his regular job and had lost their home as well, was selling cars. The car dealer gave him a "demonstrator" to drive. Tom was a year ahead of me in school and the night I walked up to school to watch him graduate, I saw the demonstrator parked on the street. I walked over to it and found his father and mother were sitting in it. I said, "Come on, let's go or you won't get a good seat."

His father said, "I can't get her to go inside."

She said to me through the window, "I don't have nice enough clothes to go in there and have all Tom's friends see me." I tried but failed to persuade her.

The Detroit Adventure

When school was out, Tom and I both looked for summer jobs. We looked until we gave up and then we talked about doing something exciting. I suggested riding a freight train to

Detroit. I said that when we got there, we could hitchhike to northern Michigan, where my aunt and uncle had a cottage on a beautiful lake, and they would be glad to see us. Tom was ready to try anything that kept him away from home.

We hitchhiked down to the railroad tracks near the Missouri River and found a group of men playing a game while they waited for a train. The game consisted of three bottle caps and a small marble the size of a pea. One man would switch the marble from one bottle cap to another in a series of fancy hand crossings. Then he would stop, sit back, and the other men would bet on which bottle cap the marble was under. We watched for quite a while until I thought I had caught on. I had five one-dollar bills and two nickels, which was a lot of money. Their slight-of-hand was better than my perception. I lost all my money except the nickels.

Suddenly, one of the men said, "Boy, are you lucky; there is a train coming along here in about ten minutes that is going to Detroit. It will be going slow up this hill and you can get on it. Tomorrow morning when it stops you will be in Detroit."

That was good enough for me. I ran three blocks to the nearest pay telephone and called my dad. He wasn't there. I left the message, "You tell my dad if I am not home for dinner, I caught a freight train for Detroit."

Five minutes after I got back to the tracks, a long freight train pulled up the hill. Tom and I dashed up to the train, grabbed the iron bars that form a ladder on the outside of a refrigerator car, and climbed to the top of the car. For the next four hours we watched the countryside wheel by and listened to the train's whistle and waved at the people. When it got dark it wasn't as much fun, and I began to get cold. All I had on my top was a short-sleeved white sweatshirt with a picture of Popeye on the front. We climbed down into the dark compartment and were amazed to find there were two men already there. I started to climb back up the ladder when one of the men said, “Sit down. There is plenty of room for four in here.”

It was so dark in there I couldn’t see his face, but I could tell by his voice that he was black. We sat on the floor with our backs against the sides. The hatch was propped open, and I could see the stars. Just before I fell asleep, I remembered that I hadn’t had anything to eat since breakfast.

When I awoke, I could see daylight through the open hatch. The train had stopped. The black man climbed up the ladder toward the blue sky and we followed.

“Is this Detroit?”

“Nope.”

“How do you know?”

“It says East St. Louis on that water tank there.”

We found another train heading the direction we were going and went to Centralia, Illinois, then on to Paducah, Kentucky. I was getting really hungry, and we were both really dirty. I took my Popeye sweatshirt off and turned it inside out.

I found a train full of coal that was going to Chicago. That wasn’t as good as Detroit, but it was the right direction. The coal train got to Blue Island, Illinois, a suburb of Chicago. When we got off we were covered with coal dust; Tom looked like he was in a minstrel show.

We were told to hike to Hammond, Indiana and catch a freight going east to Detroit. At Hammond we found a house near the tracks where a woman gave us a fried egg sandwich to eat, and green apples. The apples made us sick. Then we caught the afternoon freight train out of town. About nine o’clock in the evening, the train stopped in Kalamazoo,

Michigan. We bummed a ride into town, spent the night at the YMCA and the next morning had breakfast of oatmeal and bread in a Federal Bread Line with other transients.

Out of Kalamazoo we rode between two cars on a passenger train. The wind was rushing by us. The train would blow its whistle, and we thought we were really living.

At Battle Creek we changed trains, and rode outside a mail car. The platform was more substantial, and safer. We flew through southern Michigan.

The next stop was Jackson, Michigan. We rode in an empty freight car with several other travelers. There was an 11-year-old boy who said he hadn't had anything to eat for six days except a banana.

It was dark when the train stopped in the outskirts of Detroit, and we got off and started walking. There is a lot of walking connected with riding freight trains. We found a filling station that was open, and I asked the attendant if we could use his phone book. He looked me over and said, "You can use the phone book if you don't go in the rest room."

I looked up my Uncle Bruce Winkworth's address in the phone book and asked the attendant where it was from here. He said it was on the other side of Detroit about twenty-five miles away. He said, "Take the streetcar downtown. Then transfer to the Jefferson car and go for miles."

We walked to the end of the streetcar line. There were half a dozen people waiting for the streetcar. Tom and I started asking each one for a nickel to ride the streetcar. They all turned us down. Streetcars came and went. Among the people who waited for the next car was a red-faced man who had been drinking. He had his girlfriend with him. After a long sad story, he gave me a quarter. We were in.

It was a long streetcar ride, but we were exhilarated. It was after midnight when we found my uncle's address. I had never been there before. This was my mother's brother Bruce and his wife, Dorothy. They had one son, Brucie, who was a year younger than I. The house was dark, and I knocked on the front door. I knocked louder and louder. Finally, a window upstairs opened, and Uncle Bruce stuck his head out.

"Who is it? What is it?"

"I am David Hawley from Kansas City."

"Oh, my God." The window slammed shut. We waited a long, long time. Finally, the front door opened, and there was Uncle Bruce and Aunt Dorothy in their bathrobes. They looked at us in disbelief. It was not a warm reception.

I told them who Tom was, and they told us to go out in the backyard and take all our clothes off. Uncle Bruce brought us a cake of soap and a garden hose. After we got the first layer of dirt and coal dust off, they brought us some clothes and let us in the kitchen. When we told them how long it had been since we had eaten, Uncle Bruce went to a hamburger stand and brought us a sack full of hamburgers. We could eat very little. Tom and I both called our folks, and they were very relieved to hear from us. We went to bed in a real bed with clean sheets.

The next morning when I asked about young Brucie, I learned that he had gone away to camp. I had no way of knowing that they had sent him to camp early that morning before we woke up and corrupted him.

When Tom talked to his father on the telephone, his father told him that Tom had a cousin who was a purser on a large boat that ran between Buffalo and Detroit. Tom and I went down to the boat terminal and sure enough, the boat was in.

Tom found his cousin, who took us to lunch and gave Tom a job. I never saw Tom Bierly again.

I called my Uncle Bill Harris, who picked me up at my Uncle Bruce's house. He drove me to his house on the fabulous lake in northern Michigan that had been my original destination. I had been there many times, and my aunt and uncle were glad to see me. I extended my carefree youth one more summer. My mother and dad eventually drove up from Kansas City and took me home.

A High School Senior Like No Other

I turned sixteen before school started my Senior year in high school, and it made a good life better. My father had a 1929 Essex Super Six, and he was very generous about letting me use it. I drove it to fraternity meetings, dances and dates. The car was seven years old and had a lot of miles on it. It was a four-door, and the front seat was hinged to the floor in front. When I asked my father if I could use the car for a date, he said, "Dave, I make my living with that car. I don't have a dime's worth of insurance on it. If you wreck it, I am out of business. If you want it, take it." I took it, but I was careful.

Ward Archer lived across the street from me and was a good friend. He was six months older than I and a year ahead of me in school. Our mothers were friends and competitors.

My mother, Mrs. Archer and I went to Ward's graduation. Ward was a good student and active in several school activities. He received due recognition for which Mrs. Archer bragged to my mother on the way home. My mother replied that she didn't understand why Ward didn't sit on the stage. Mrs. Archer explained to my mother that with a graduating class of almost five hundred, only representative students — six boys and six girls—could sit on the stage.

My mother said that she thought that I would probably sit on the stage when I graduated. Mrs. Archer kindly didn't say anything. When we got home, my mother said to me, "Now, David, I seldom ask anything of you" (this was her standard beginning) "but I am asking you now, in plenty of time. I want you to sit on the stage when you graduate." She didn't care how I got there. She just wanted to one-up Mrs. Archer.

In the first week of school my Senior year, I went down to Mr. Bryan's office, requested an interview, and said, "Mr. Bryan, I would like to sit on the stage when I graduate. You tell me what I have to do to do it, and I will see if it is possible."

Mr. Bryan looked at me for a while and said, "That is not a position you volunteer for. The people on the stage are members of the Senior Business Committee. It is made up of the leaders in the various activities of the school. Offhand, I don't see how you could possibly qualify for this."

I thanked him and went on my way. About ten days later, in my homeroom, I got a message to report for a meeting after school in Mr. Bryan's office. When all twelve people arrived, I found myself among the head jocks and brains of the Senior class. Mr. Bryan told us we had been selected as the members of the Senior Business Committee. We would hold a dinner meeting at one of the hotels once a month until we graduated. The purpose of the meetings would be to discuss and act upon the business of the Senior Class. They set the date for the first meeting and adjourned.

Mr. Bryan asked me to stay for a minute. After everyone was gone, he said, "Now, Dave, you got what you asked for. I am telling you now, you must be one-hundred percent cooperative with me and the school this year. The first time a teacher sends you to my office for discipline, you are off the Senior Business Committee, and the stage. Have you got it?"

I said, "Yes, I got it." As I walked home that night, I said to myself, I got it, but I am not sure I want it.

The first football game was played about a month later. It was at Paseo High School, and I was sitting with a group of my fraternity brothers fairly high up in the bleachers. We were kidding around, acting silly and being loud. A girl said to me, "Please sit down, David. Mr. Bryan is sitting over there watching you and getting madder and madder."

It never occurred to me we were making anybody mad. I thought everybody was enjoying it. On Monday morning, I received a note in my homeroom to report to Mr. Bryan's office. He started in, "When people go to a football game, they go to watch the game." He went on a long rampage and said, "Dave, you know what I told you about being in my office."

I said, "Mr. Bryan, you said the first time a teacher sent me down here. No teacher sent me down here." After another long tirade, he said, "All right. This is your last chance to sit on that stage. You got it?"

I said, "Yes, I got it."

There were other opportunities for me to get into trouble; about once a month, I got "one more chance" throughout my Senior year. When I graduated, I sat on the stage. My mother and father were proud. Mr. Bryan was proud. I was proud. I think even Mrs. Archer was proud.

When December came, there was a dance every Friday and Saturday night. I was in love with two girls, and they both responded to my attention. One Saturday night, there was a dance at Mission Hills Country Club, to which I was invited by Olivia O'Brien. I double-dated with Billy Shofstall. Billy's father suggested we take his car since we usually drove my dad's car. He also said he wanted me to drive, since Billy was not yet sixteen and didn't have a driver's license. He had a new red Oldsmobile with twenty-two hundred miles on it. It was a big change from my dad's seven-year-old Essex.

It was a bad night for a new driver with snow and ice on the side streets. We picked up our dates and went to a wonderful party. It was a cut-in dance with a lot of stags. Olivia was very popular, and I almost had to stand in line to dance with her. I had the keys to that new Oldsmobile in my pocket, and the temptation was too great. I thought I would take it for a spin around the block and be back before Olivia or Billy missed me.

As I was going out the front door, a boy leaning there that I hardly knew, Frank something or other, asked to go with me. After I had driven around a couple blocks, I had a brilliant thought. My other girlfriend, Suzy Stocking, was sitting at home. She hadn't been invited to the dance. I could run by her house and say hello.

I was driving down a side street too fast when I lost control on the ice. I hit the brakes. I glanced off a parked car, slid sideways and ran into a tree with the right side of the Oldsmobile. I hit my head against the ventilator window. The tree was in somebody's front yard. The people had been playing cards, and they came pouring out, as did the neighbors. I was standing there in my tuxedo, no overcoat, rather dazed, with Frank something or other, who had obviously been drinking.

The man whose front yard I was in owned the car I hit. He said to me, "Well, what are you going to do about it?"

It was a modest neighborhood in the heart of the Depression, and I think Frank and I represented something these people didn't care for. The second time this man asked me, "Well, what are you going to do about it?" I answered, "I guess I better call my dad. Can I use your phone?"

The man looked at me as if he hated me and said, "I wouldn't want you in my house. You can use the public phone at the drug store."

The drug store was only a few doors down the street. I called my dad at home. I said, "I was driving Billy Shofstall's father's car tonight and I had a wreck."

"Was anybody hurt?"

"No."

"Will the car run?"

"No."

"Call the Brookside garage and have it hauled in."

"Before I hit the tree, I hit a parked car."

"Call the Brookside garage and have two cars hauled in."

"The guy that owns the car I hit has hold of my collar and doesn't act like he wants to turn loose."

"Where are you?"

I gave him the address. "Hold onto him. I will be right over."

When Dad got out of his car and walked up to the group, the man who had been so unfriendly started to yell. "Is this your son?"

My dad said, "Yes, this is my son. Are you the guy that had hold of him?"

My dad is not very tall, but he sounded very authoritative. The man backed off. "Calm down. He ran into my car."

My dad said, "If your car is damaged, we will have it repaired. I will have this car towed in and tell the garage they can expect you Monday morning."

Frank and I got in the Essex and Dad drove us back to our house. When we got to our house, he said, "You had better take my car and go back to the party. Olivia and Billy are going to be wondering what happened. You tell Billy I will contact his father in the morning."

When I got back to the dance, intermission had started, and Billy and his date and Olivia were all looking for me. They didn't believe me when I first told them what had happened. But they eventually did.

A couple of days later, I heard my mother ask my father what he was going to do to me for wrecking the Shofstall's car. My dad said, "Nothing. There isn't anything that you or I can say or do that will make him feel any worse or us feel any better."

With the exception of a few minor problems like Mr. Bryan and the Shofstall's car, my Senior year in high school was a great success. I sat on the stage at graduation and decided that I represented all the mediocre people in the class.

CHAPTER 2
HIGHER EDUCATION

Calling Western Union

After graduation, it was absolutely essential that I get work for the summer. I got a job as a Western Union messenger boy. I was fitted for my uniform and took a short course in looking neat and speaking respectfully. I worked out of the main Kansas City office at Seventh and Walnut Street from two in the afternoon until eleven at night. We were paid by the number of telegrams we delivered and how far we carried them. Telegrams were much cheaper than long distance phone calls, and most offices had a direct buzzer to the Western Union office to call a messenger to pick up telegrams.

At six o'clock, the branch Western Union offices closed, and we covered the whole city. No messages were telephoned; they were all hand delivered. I either walked or rode my bicycle to all the big hotels, but the small crummy hotels were the place where my education was furthered.

I went to the West Bottoms down the Twelfth Street viaduct many times. I covered the City Market on Fifth Street. And I went to all the night clubs. One of my fellow workers was an Italian boy whose older sister was a striptease dancer on Twelfth Street. Her brother knew her schedule, and he and I would watch her show first at one club and then another. She had an appendicitis scar, and I got so I could recognize her anywhere.

One of my most interesting assignments came one night when we got a call to send a messenger to the Bar Le Duc nightclub on Twelfth Street. The manager of the nightclub had a letter that he wanted delivered to the lady who was the star in the Gillis Burlesque theater. The Gillis was on Walnut between Fourth and Fifth. He said, "I want this letter handed to her personally. I don't care how long it takes. Wait for an answer."

When I got to the Gillis, the ticket seller said he would deliver the letter for me. I said, "Nothing doing!" I had to deliver it myself and wait for an answer. The theater was about half full. When I opened the door to the dressing room, I found the star with a couple other ladies waiting their turn to go on, and two baggy-pants comedians. When I handed her the letter, I told her I was supposed to wait for an answer. She read it, and it obviously pleased her. Before she could answer it, she had to go on stage and do her number. She told me to sit down and wait.

This was a real "dressing" room: the girls took their costumes off on the stage and put them back on in here. I didn't know whether to watch the star perform or visit with the other people in the dressing room. When the star got all her clothes off on the stage, she came back in the dressing room. She put on a bathrobe and sat down to write the answer. She looked at me for a moment as though she was going to give me some profound advice. I was ready to receive it. Then she shrugged and said, "Forget it. Don't take any wooden nickels, kid."

I went back to the Bar Le Duc nightclub and delivered the letter to the manager just as the girl in his floorshow was taking her clothes off. I looked to see if she had an appendicitis scar, but she didn't. He gave me a seventy-five cent tip, which was the biggest tip I had ever received. He then told me confidentially that he had been a Western Union messenger and look where he had risen to. I went back to the main office and bragged about my adventure.

This was the summer of 1936, when the Pendergast "machine" ran Kansas City. It was a wide open town. Every nightclub on Twelfth Street had a floorshow that included a striptease dancer. They also had a crap table with a crap game in progress. There was a jazz band playing in every nightclub. Names that have since become famous, like Count Basie, were playing with no cover charge, no minimum, and no age limit. Anybody could buy a drink. No one cared how old you were.

On Twelfth Street there was also the Beatle Dance Palace. It was a dime dance hall. They advertised fifty beautiful hostesses waiting to dance with you. The first time I went in there, I was amazed at how close the girl danced to me. I loved it. I liked the way she smiled, I liked the way she smelled, and I loved the way she pressed her pelvic area against my business area. I had bought two tickets for twenty cents. When the two numbers ended, she said, "Do you want to buy some more tickets?"

I said, "Yes, I do."

She held onto my hand as I walked over to the window to buy two more tickets. I hoped that the dim lighting in the place would keep anybody from seeing the bulge in the front of my pants.

The red light district had its center at Fourteenth and Holmes. In the warm weather, the prostitutes would stand on the sidewalk and call to men driving by. The standard charge was one dollar, and the girls were friendly and pretty. The girls in that area were all white. The black girls were further east and a little cheaper. I should say "less expensive." I delivered several telegrams to a girl named Alma at 1410 Holmes. The first time I stopped there, she asked me my name and gave me a tip. She couldn't be all bad. Those girls carried cards that said they were free from venereal disease. They had to pay for those cards and have them renewed periodically. I assume they had an inspection when their cards were renewed. A policeman would check them to see that their cards were up to date.

A high school friend of mine named Maury Gower went to a basketball game at Convention Hall with his father. When they came out, their car had been broken into and their overcoats had been stolen. They went to the police station to report it. They walked by a large group of prostitutes that were waiting in line for something. One of them said, "Hi, Maury. How have you been?" The other girls, seeing his embarrassment, took it up. As they walked past the line, every other girl said, "Hi, Maury." The girls were very friendly, and they knew everybody's names.

On to College

When the summer was over, I enrolled in Kansas City Junior College at Eleventh and Locust. The Junior College was part of the Kansas City public school system. It cost twelve dollars per semester. It was just like a continuation of high school, only it was harder. Kansas City Junior College had a good academic rating. If you did well in Junior College, they claimed you could go anywhere.

My dad would have liked to send me away to school, but he just didn't have the money. He had reopened his office downtown, and business was starting to pick up, but it was awfully slow. He was still paying back the money he had borrowed in 1933 and '34.

My father went to Princeton and graduated a Phi Beta Kappa. He had always been an excellent student. I never understood why he didn't encourage me to be an excellent student. I always felt that he not only loved me like a father, but he also liked me.

Because you could live at home and go to Junior College, the school had more applicants than they could accommodate. Consequently, you couldn't fool around. You had to attend classes and pass the subjects if you wished to continue. I had always been an average student. I never worked hard at it, and the teachers who liked me usually pointed that out to me.

The week before school started, Mrs. Neenan called my mother and said they were hiring ushers for the new Music Hall that was getting ready to open. Her son Jimmy and our mutual friend, Billy McGonigal, had already been hired. I should be sure and tell the interviewer that I was a student at Rockhurst College. Neither Jimmy Neenan or Billy McGonigal went to Rockhurst, but they were both good Catholics, and that, I am sure, is how they heard about the job. I immediately went down and applied. When the man asked me where I went to school, I told him Rockhurst, and he followed that up with questions about a couple of the Fathers out there. I didn't know the answers, and I didn't get the job. I immediately went out to Rockhurst and found out which Father did what. The next day I went back to the Music Hall and got the job. The manager of the Music Hall was George Goldman, a Jew, and I thought it unusual that he would be the one that required the ushers to all be Catholics. I suppose he had received that suggestion from someone higher up. Pendergast was a Catholic.

The job was a real plum. To start with, they paid us two dollars and fifty cents a night, and that was a lot of money in 1936. In addition to the money, we saw all the best plays and concerts. There was something there almost every night. The Philharmonic Orchestra played two identical concerts Wednesday and Thursday nights every two weeks. I kept that job for the two years I went to Junior College, and by the end of the two years, I actually enjoyed the Philharmonic. You had to wear a tuxedo on this job, and they all had to be alike. That meant I had to buy a new one. At seventeen, I got my second tuxedo.

The Junior College was located on the eastern edge of downtown. There was no campus, no beautiful buildings, no trees. If we had an hour when we weren't in school, we played pool in one of the pool halls on Tenth Street. The Greek that owned the restaurant where we ate lunch made me an offer. The lunches were twenty-five cents. He said if I would bring my friends with me when I came, I would get my lunch for fifteen cents. It was a good lunch, and we ate there a lot.

The manager of the YMCA called me to come see him. He had a proposition. The YMCA at Tenth and Oak had a big gym, a nice swimming pool, a track and an exercise room. And no one using it in the afternoons. It cost twenty-five dollars to join the YMCA, but he would let the boys from Junior College join for five dollars each. They even had pool tables at the YMCA. This would get them out of the pool halls on the street and give the YMCA a little income. My membership would be free. My friends welcomed the idea, and we all started spending our afternoons at the YMCA. We played basketball, boxed and swam. It was a great deal. You had to pay a nickel for a towel.

Construction workers were finishing the new building for the City Hall across the street to the west from Junior College. One morning when my dad drove me to school, he said that he had tried to sell them a revolving door for both entrances to the new building. He said that due to the fact the foyer on the first floor was several stories high, there would be a tremendous updraft when the weather got cold. He said it would take a lot of strength to open the outside swinging doors because there would be so much pressure on them on a real cold morning. When we were studying heat in my Physics class, I told the class this theory as if it were my own. Everyone made fun of me, including the teacher. He said when they build a big building like that, they have engineers that figure things like that out. They didn't know about my dad.

My dad was a graduate civil engineer, one of the best. But he had decided years ago that while the engineers got all the responsibility, the men selling the materials made the money. He was a manufacturer's agent and represented thirteen manufacturers. The contractors, engineers, and architects all called him for information about the products he sold. He really made his living giving out free information and advice. In return, they specified or bought his products.

It turned cold suddenly that year, and we had a big temperature drop one night. The next morning when I went to school, there was a large group standing in front of the City Hall seeing who was strong enough to open the swinging doors with the cold air trying to get in. My Physics class, including the teacher, looked on me with new respect. The City immediately bought two revolving doors from my dad.

My father liked to make his own wine. He was extremely proud of his wine, and he would serve it before Sunday dinner and on holidays. He would often irritate my mother by not coming in to sit down when the dinner was ready. He wanted to complete the story he was telling or the poem he was reciting, and finish his wine. He called his wine "Old Doctor Hawley's Speedy Specific," and when my mother would say, "The dinner is ready," my father would say, "Let's have one more glass of Speedy Specific."

At the Thanksgiving dinner that year, we had the Upjohns for company, plus my sister Harriett's new boyfriend. The cocktail hour lasted longer than usual. The "Speedy Specific" was better than ever. My mother didn't take part; she didn't care for the wine. She had heard all those poems before, and she was busy in the kitchen. She called for us to come to the dinner table several times before Dad reluctantly released his audience. We all sat down, and Dad said the grace. He started to carve the beautiful turkey. Just as my mother came through the pantry door with a big bowl of mashed potatoes, my father said, "Lucille has never learned that the food is not the most important part of Thanksgiving." Mother turned the bowl of mashed potatoes upside down on top of Dad's head. Some of the potatoes went on his shoulders and arms and in his lap. She removed the bowl and some of the potatoes stayed on his head. He never said a word, but continued to carve the turkey. The children busted out laughing, then Mr. and Mrs. Upjohn, and finally, my mother. My dad continued to carve the turkey.

Sunday dinner was an important event at our house every week. It was a big feast, and we spent half of the afternoon eating it. My father only allowed one conversation at a time at our dinner table. Everyone listened to whomever had the floor. Mr. and Mrs. Upjohn were very often our Sunday dinner guests, and many Sundays when we were younger, we would go for a long ride in their LaSalle after dinner. Harriett and I would sit in the jump seats. We both hated it. By the time we got to Junior College, we had graduated from the jump seats and didn't have to take the rides.

My second year in Junior College, I was still playing pool, eating lunch at the Cortez lunch room for fifteen cents, working out at the YMCA, and ushering almost every night. My first class in the morning was an English class, and I sat in the back row next to a girl named Alice.

Alice worked at the Tower Theatre on Twelfth Street and was a dancer, a "Tower Adorable." The Tower had a floorshow in between movies with big time stars like Cab Callaway that performed there.

Alice worked every night and didn't always get her homework done. One morning she showed up looking very tired and with some of her "Tower Adorable" makeup still on. I told her I thought we were going to have a quiz, and asked her if she needed any help. She said, "Oh, yes. I haven't read any of the material. I didn't make it home last night."

I got to where I could tell from the amount of makeup she still had on whether Alice had made it home the night before. Alice was a dancer, and she had a terrific body. When I thought about what her activities might have been from the time she left the Tower Theatre until she arrived at our English class in the morning, I couldn't think about English.

You had to have a C average to graduate from Junior College. I went there for four semesters. The first three semesters, I made all C's. The fourth and last semester, I made a D in Physics. The teacher couldn't understand how a student who was bright enough to figure out that the architects and engineers had put the wrong doors in the new City Hall could make a D on the semester exam. This D kept me from graduating. Fortunately, my parents didn't know there was a graduating exercise from such a lowly thing as Junior College. They didn't know that Junior College gave a degree. It was a good thing they didn't know, because I didn't get one.

I planned to go to the University of Missouri at Columbia (M. U.) for my Junior year. Many of my high school friends were there, and I would fit right in. A week before school started, I visited a friend of mine, Gene Amick, at William Jewell College in Liberty, Missouri. I was tremendously impressed with his friends, boys who seemed to care more about that school and that fraternity than I had ever cared about anything. Their enthusiasm was more than I could resist. William Jewell was a Baptist college, and my whole family were Baptists. When I went home and told my folks that I wanted to go to William Jewell, they were amazed. My dad said, "We would love to have you go to William Jewell, but I don't think you will like it. I think you would be better off to go to M.U. where your friends are and there are more people like you."

Nevertheless, I enrolled in William Jewell, and after about six weeks, I decided my dad was right. It was too late to quit, so I made the best of it.

The boys at William Jewell were mostly from small towns. Many of their fathers were successful businessmen who may have owned the picture show, the funeral parlor, the lumberyard, or maybe the Ford dealership. They were the only ones from small towns who felt they could send their sons to college in times as hard as these. In the City where I grew up, everybody went to college. No matter how broke they were at home, it would be socially unacceptable not to get a college education.

When I entered William Jewell as a Junior, I had to decide on a major for my course of study. I asked my father what he suggested. He said he had no idea what I was going to do for a living, but he knew I wasn't going to be an engineer. He said his parents had spent so much money educating him to be an engineer that he felt he had to be one, although economic circumstances dictated otherwise. He said everybody should take four years of mathematics because that taught you to think. Other than the math, he didn't care what I took, but he thought I should major in something at which I knew I couldn't make a living. He said that way I would be free to do whatever came naturally.

I decided to major in English Literature. I enjoyed it. It was easy for me, and I knew I couldn't make a living at it.

The second week of school was Rush Week for the fraternities. Liberty was only thirty miles from Kansas City, so the fraternity that was rushing me, Phi Gamma Delta, took me and a group of rushees to dinner and a nightclub in K.C. Most of the rushees were naive Freshmen but I had grown up in this town. We went to a nightclub where they had an orchestra and a floorshow. The star of the floorshow was a pretty blond who sang and danced. She was greatly appreciated by our group. When the show was over, we were standing in line at the hat check booth when the blond bombshell from the floorshow walked across the lobby. She saw me and squealed, "Davey!" She ran up, threw her arms around my neck, and gave me a big kiss right on the mouth. It was Alice from my English class at Junior College. Not only were the other rushees impressed, the active members who were our hosts felt they had a real find in me. My reputation was made. Alice had graduated from her place in the chorus line at the Tower Adorables. In her upward mobility, she had carried me with her. I was easily elected president of the pledge class. I was also chosen a cheerleader for the Pep Rallies and football games

William Jewell College in 1938 and '39 was right out of a Bing Crosby college movie. We had pep rallies, football games, homecoming parades, fraternity dances, and lots of fraternity spirit. The academic end of it was easy for me; it was easier than Junior College. I was majoring in English Literature, and I had a good background. I ate my meals in the fraternity house and lived in the annex across the street. If I didn't have anything to do in the evening, I went to the library and walked a pretty girl home to her dormitory. You couldn't beat it.

Very few students had automobiles, and the price of a Coke or a candy bar was about the extent of their disposable income. I had a job working on weekends, but I wasn't rich like I was in Junior College.

I finished my Junior year and floated into my Senior year. Now I was the head cheerleader, which made me the master of ceremonies at pep rallies and other miscellaneous gatherings where it was important to show school spirit.

A couple days before school started my Senior year, I was in town helping the brothers do a little advance rushing and decided to go swimming in the school's indoor pool. The only other occupants of the pool were a half a dozen Freshmen. I recognized that three of them were from Carrollton, Missouri. I had been going with a girl from Carrollton, and I had gone down there and visited her and stayed at the family house that summer. I had met all the young people in Carrollton, and I was anxious that these Freshmen carry a good report of me back to their home town.

I decided to show off for them. The pool had a balcony from which spectators could view the swimming meets. The front of the balcony had a low cement wall that was topped by a round steel railing. I stood on the railing and prepared to dive. When I knew I had everybody's attention, I sprang. Unfortunately, my right foot was still a little wet. It slipped off and didn't give me the push I needed. I never made it to the water: I landed on the tile below.

I pulled myself up to a sitting position and said, "Don't worry about it. It happens all the time." I assured them I was all right and would just sit there until I got my breath back. I scooted myself over to the wall to lean against. I had landed on my shoulder and my back, but what hurt were my legs and my feet. I had one of the students go to the fraternity house and have someone come and get me. I couldn't walk back home. Fortunately, my injuries were minor.

Dr. F. T. Walker

The head of English department was Dr. Franklin Trenelby Walker. He was a man of early middle age with graying hair and gray mustache. He was a studious man with a Southern accent who appeared to me to be naïve and insecure. He once told me that the owner of the grocery store where he charged his groceries came to his back door and asked him to pay his bill, which was overdue. He thought college professors should be treated with more respect.

In my Junior year, I had a course under Dr. Walker, and we didn't get along too well. I made the mistake of sitting in the back of the room. There were some noisy boys in the back row who made remarks that made the class laugh. Dr. Walker was near-sighted and couldn't tell who was doing it. I had the face and the attitude that went with the remarks, so he blamed it on me. As a consequence, he surprised me by giving me a D for a semester grade. I couldn't stand this, because a D in your major doesn't count toward graduation.

I went to the Dean of Men, Dean Moon, and complained that I had been unfairly treated. After a three-way conference, Dean Moon asked Dr. Walker to give me an oral examination in his presence. And he did. We had been studying Shakespeare, and poor Dr. Walker picked Hamlet to be the subject of the oral test. The two previous years when I had attended Junior College in Kansas City and ushered at the Music Hall, I had seen the play Hamlet several times. The first year, Hamlet ran two weeks with Maurice Edwards playing the unhappy hero, and the second year it ran three weeks with Leslie Howard as the star.

When Dr. Walker asked the questions about the play, I answered them as if I had written it. Dr. Walker and Dean Moon were both impressed. Dr. Walker was also embarrassed. He gave me a better grade, but he still didn't love me.

He was the only one who taught fourth year English Literature, so I had to take his course my Senior year. That first day, Dr. Walker gave us a little lecture. He said, "If there is any talent in this school in the field of English, it has to be among the students in this room. The only chance an English professor like me has to succeed is to have students who are capable of appreciating him. The English professors who have become famous did so on the basis of what their students carried away from their classrooms. If during the course of this series of classes, I should say something that you think is particularly to the point or worth remembering, I wish that you would jot it down. Put some three-by-five cards in your book so you won't write in your book. Maybe you would like to show me the cards when the course is over."

As the course progressed, I thought I did as well as anybody. But I didn't jot anything down on a three-by-five card. Some of the uninspired girls in the class sat there and wrote down everything he said. The day before the examination, Dr. Walker described what the examination consisted of, and when he finished, he said, "By the way, if you have any of the three-by-five cards on which you made notes, bring them with you to the examination. I would like to see them."

I knew I was in trouble. But I hoped my grade on the examination would make up for my lack of "appreciation" cards. The examination, it turned out, was no big deal. When you finished, you went through a door at the rear of the room where Dr. Walker stood. You handed him your examination, and if you had any cards, you handed those to him also. He would look at them and hand them back to you.

When I finished the exam, I walked to the rear of the room and handed him my paper. I didn't hand him any cards to look at.

"No cards, Mr. Hawley?"

I didn't say anything. With his eyes on my paper, Dr. Walker said, "During this entire semester you didn't hear anything that you thought was worth remembering."

I couldn't stand the pressure. I turned coward and said, "Oh, I made plenty of notes, Dr. Walker, but they aren't very neat; they aren't organized, and at the last minute, I forgot them. I remembered them before I came into class, but I thought they weren't worth going back after."

Dr. Walker kept his eyes on my test paper as he said, "Mr. Hawley, I would like to see those cards. I will be in my office until two o'clock. That ought to give you plenty of time to bring them up here."

I lived in Mrs. Kirby's boarding house. It was across the street from the Phi Gam House and used for the overflow. I bought some index cards on the way home. I retired to my room and started putting some of Dr. Walker's smart sayings on the cards. At the end of several cards, I ran out of smart sayings. If I had handed him the four cards when I walked out of the exam room I might have gotten away with it. But after the big build- up, it would look like I had gone to my room and written them. I thought about it, and decided to take a chance. I went down to Mrs. Kirby's kitchen where she had a wooden box filled with file cards. Every card had a different recipe written in neat longhand. I took a stack about an inch high and put the four cards I had written on top. I put a strong rubber band around the package and headed for Dr. Walker's office.

I had watched him as he had handled the other students' stack of cards. He would read the top card and riffle the deck with his thumb. Quantity was what he was interested in. He sometimes didn't even read the top card. He would then hand them back and say, "Very good, Miss Jones."

When I knocked, he said, "Come in." He was alone.

I held out my stack of cards, and he said, "Sit down."

I was seated across a small desk from him. He read the top card and appeared to think for a minute. Then, he pulled the top card off and read the second card. He riffled through the deck with his thumb and he said, "Very good, Mr. Hawley. This shows that you really grasped the idea I was trying to put across."

I reached my hand out for the cards, but instead of handing them to me, he thumped the end of the deck on his desk.

He looked back at the top card in front of him, and he said, "I have a confession to make, Mr. Hawley. When you said you had left your cards at home, I didn't think you had any cards. It just further points up that you and I have not understood one another. We got off on the wrong foot last year, and I have always felt that you were resisting my efforts."

He was obviously embarrassed and nervous. While he talked, he was fumbling with my stack of cards. He would pull one out of the center of the pack about an inch and shove it back in. He finally looked up at me and said, "I have looked over your exam, and you have done well. You know the material. Fortunately, we have another semester ahead of us in which we can have an honest relationship and appreciate one another."

At this point, he pulled one of the cards all the way out of the pack. As he continued to talk about how he had misjudged me, he had the pack of cards in one hand and the individual card from the middle of the pack in the other hand. I reached for the pack, and when I did, he tried to insert the card back into the pack. At this point, he held it up where he could read it. It was a recipe for Plum Pudding. He stopped and appeared to think, as if he were trying to fit Plum Pudding into the course he was teaching.

When he pulled the second card out of the middle of the pack and read that recipe, he got an incredulous look on his face and pulled out another card, and another. I reached over and took the stack of cards and the loose ones on his desk.

"I will need to return these cards," I said. Then I walked out and shut the door. I returned Mrs. Kirby's recipe cards to her wooden box and went up to my room and started to pack.

Dr. Walker didn't ask me to be punished. But he said I couldn't be in any more of his classes. Since he was the only one who taught the English course I needed to graduate, there was no point in my continuing. I went home that night and told my father I had decided to quit school. He never asked me why I was quitting in the middle of my Senior year. He said I could go to work for him starting the next morning. And so I entered the exciting world of the toilet partition business.

Toilet Partitions et al

Actually, my dad sold other things besides toilet partitions. As a manufacturer's agent, he sold revolving doors, elevator doors, fire doors, escalators, steel casement windows, and several other things. When I went to work for him, he had no other employees. I started out typing his letters and answering the phone when he was out.

Sometimes he sent me on a selling assignment, and when I came back to the office, he would make me repeat the whole conversation with the customer. When it came to the "turn down" and the buyer said he wasn't interested, my dad would say, "Did you tell him about the so and so or this good feature?"

If I said no, he would say, "Go back and tell him about it."

When I returned the second time, I would repeat the conversation, and if I had left out any of the sale talk or the features, my dad would send me back a third time. I soon learned to give the prospect the whole story the first time. It was much easier than going back a second and a third time. When my dad was out of the office and I was there answering the phone, I sometimes took a nap on the library table that held literature. We left our door standing open, and several people surprised me in that position. My dad said I was the only person he knew that could spend the day gazing out the window and be perfectly happy.

About 1940, I got an additional employer. H. R. Farnum was a food broker on the floor above us. He needed someone to write his letters. I had plenty of time and could use the extra money. Mr. Farnum, who was quite a bit older than my dad, sold peas, peanuts, and caviar. When making a sales call, Mr. Farnum always talked to the head man. Mr. Farnum had been at this business a long time, and when he called up Wolferman's store, he asked for Fred Wolferman. When he called Milgram's store, he talked to Mr. Milgram. They all knew H. R. Farnum, and he sold them a world of peas, peanuts, and caviar.

Mr. Farnum wore a derby hat and carried a cane. He got a shave and a shoe shine every morning at the Muehlebach Hotel. He rode the streetcar, and when he was waiting for it, he would step between the tracks and wave his cane as if he were waving down a fast passenger train. No matter how many people were waiting for the streetcar, or how early he had arrived, Mr. Farnum was the last one to get on. Sometimes when he would come in with a letter for me to write, he would have a jar of caviar and a loaf of bread. We would have a caviar sandwich. When he called his wife on the telephone, he always addressed her as Mrs. Farnum. He would say, "Mrs. Farnum, this is H. R. Farnum. Has the mail come in yet?"

I worked for C. S. Hawley Company one full year and went back to William Jewell and started in right where I had quit. I went to see Professor Walker before I enrolled and told him what a terrible price I had paid for my deception with the recipe cards. I was very contrite, and he agreed to allow me to enter his class in Senior English. I moved into the fraternity house and roomed with Gene Amick and Robert Strickland.

That last semester in college was the only time during my college career that I made good grades. It was also the only time that I did not work at a job. I also did not have the distractions of an active social life.

In the last week of school, the head of every department took one graduating Senior to a fancy dinner. It was a recognition for a student who had majored in his department and done well. Dr. Walker invited me. At the dinner, the professors rose one at a time and introduced their guests. I sat there waiting, knowing that every professor there knew about the recipe cards I had turned in. When it came his turn, Professor Walker and I stood up and for a moment, I thought he had forgotten my name. When he finally said my name, I was sure the applause was definitely louder than it had been for anyone else. I thought, They are clapping for him for being broadminded enough to bring me. Nobody liked him before, but now he's a hero.

CHAPTER 3
NAVY MAN

The Navy Air Corps

I graduated from college the end of May in 1941 and immediately joined the Navy Air Corps. I joined it for two reasons: I wanted to prove I could pass the physical, and I wanted to please my father. My dad had not been in World War One. His age and his family position made him eligible to miss it, and he chose to do so. He always felt that he missed out and regretted it. He wasn't going to have this happen to me.

When I came home and said I had passed the physical and had been sworn in, he was happy as could be. I started immediately in basic training. The first day, we had marching, ground school, and went for our first airplane ride. I had never been up in an airplane before.

Most of the flight instructors were commercial airline pilots who had learned to fly in the Navy and now were being called back in to help build a bigger air force. I didn't think they were too enthusiastic about the job. The basic trainers were yellow biplanes. They were called "The Yellow Menace." My problem was I couldn't reach the pedals. At the end of the runway, you held your feet on the brakes while you warmed up the motor. If I slid down in the seat far enough to put enough pressure on the brakes to hold the plane still, I was out of position to fly the plane. To taxi the plane, you steered it by putting pressure on one foot brake and partially releasing the other. I couldn't sit up and do it. My instructor wasn't very patient with me. The United States was not in the war, and we didn't have a very military atmosphere. Most of the other students were boys who had spent their whole lives being in love with airplanes. They had started out building model airplanes and sent in the box tops for the Flight Commander's pin. When a plane flew over, they could identify it and describe it. This was not the case with me.

At the end of six weeks, we soloed. My instructor had been very critical of me, so I wasn't surprised when I was included in the large group to be reevaluated. A group of officers spent two days interviewing these "questionables" to see if they should be allowed to continue in the program. It was a traumatic experience for many of these young men for whom flying was the only important thing in their lives. It was hard on the officers doing the interviewing also.

I was one of the very last to be interviewed. While I was waiting in the anteroom, I talked to the yeoman who kept the records. He was a boy from my high school named Harley Barth. I had known Harley a long time, and I asked him to look at the records and see if it would do me any good to go in there and ask them for another chance. Harley said, "Many of these fellows are being given another chance. But your record is so bad they won't give you another chance under any circumstances."

Soon after that, I was called into the room. Seated around a long directors' table was a group of tired, depressed Naval officers. The four-stripe captain at the end of the table said, "All right, son, tell us whose fault it was that you have these 'down' marks on your flying record."

I said, "It wasn't anybody's fault, sir. I did my best to learn how to fly. The instructors did their best to teach me how. This just doesn't seem to be my thing, but there was no way of knowing this until we tried."

The officers around the table all looked up and smiled. The captain acted amazed. He said, "You are the first one today to have an intelligent attitude about this. We aren't going to let you fly anymore, but we certainly want you to stay in the Navy. You can pick your school: navigator, bombardier, etc."

I said, "I deeply appreciate your offer, but I would prefer to receive a discharge and return to civilian status."

I was discharged the next day. When I started emptying my locker and packing my clothes, my friends came around to tell me how sorry they were that I was leaving. I said, "Not to worry. There are so many things in this world that I do well, it would be foolish of me to continue to do something that I do poorly, especially when I might end up doing it against somebody who is playing hardball."

As I rode the bus home, I tried to convince myself that this was true. I had a hard time thinking of anything I did well.

I didn't get a hero's welcome when I got home. My father was terribly disappointed. I didn't tell him I couldn't reach the pedals. I knew he wouldn't accept that. He kept saying, "You are extremely intelligent. You are very well-coordinated. I just can't understand it." I started looking for another way to join the Armed Services and make my father happy.

One of my friends had joined the Navy's V-7 program. It was a four-month course for college graduates. When you graduated at the end of four months, you were given a commission as a deck officer in the Navy. I went down and applied. This was six months before Pearl Harbor. The officer that interviewed me said the Navy had all the deck officers they needed. They had a long list of young men waiting to get into the program. The only openings they had were for engineering officers. He looked over my college transcript and due to my father's insistence that I take four years of college Math and Physics, he was impressed. He said if I only had a year of Chemistry he could get me in the program. It was a four-month school and when you graduated you were a commissioned officer in the engine room.

I started looking for a quick way to get a year of Chemistry. After several inquiries, I found that at Rockhurst College, a Jesuit school in Kansas City, they said they would give me credit for a year of Chemistry as soon as I completed the laboratory work and could pass the comprehensive examination. The Father who was the head of the department said he would tutor me for an hourly fee that was very reasonable. I started looking for a night job that would pay for the tutoring. I got a job running the elevator at the Netherlands Hotel at Thirty-ninth and Main Street. I wore a uniform that was right out of the movies and worked from four o'clock in the afternoon until midnight.

At the end of six weeks, I finished Chemistry and made an A on the examination. They added this to my transcript, and I returned to the Navy. When I took the physical, they said I wasn't tall enough or heavy enough. I stood up taller, ate six bananas, and they swore me in. I was now in the Naval Reserve, and they would call me as soon as there was an opening. The date was December 1, 1941—six days before Pearl Harbor.

I had quit my job at the Netherlands Hotel. I was out of money, and I didn't know how long it would be before the Navy called me. Mr. Chaffee, from my church, said he could get me an interim job at the Sheffield Steel Mill if I didn't care what I did. I had some classmates who had gone to work in the office at Sheffield Steel. I thought if I started in the Mill at the bottom, I would not only get in good physical condition, I would also see how long it would take for my abilities to be recognized without the competition of other college graduates.

Sheffield Steel & The Nut Line

I started on the Nut Line at Sheffield Steel. My job was to stand facing a revolving hollow metal cone. I had a barrel of nuts on one side and a barrel of bolts on the other. I started the nut onto the bolt with my fingers. Then I stuck the nut into the interior of the revolving cone while I held onto the bolt. This spun the nut farther onto the bolt. I threw this bolt and nut into a third barrel and picked up another bolt and another nut. I continued this operations until I got to the bottom of one of the barrels. When I thrust the nut into the cone, I would have hold of the bolt, including the square head of the bolt. If for some reason, the nut didn't turn, the square bolt head would spin in the palm of my hand. At the end of the first day, I was not only exhausted, there was no skin left in the palm of my right hand. The next day, I taped my right hand and wore a leather glove over it.

We were paid by the number of barrels we had completed the day before. On the morning of my second day, I saw my name with "$5.50" after it, the minimum. I said to one of my fellow workers that I sure was slow in catching on. He replied, "You can't expect to learn a skill like this overnight."

My shift started at seven in the morning. I rode the bus downtown and transferred to the Twelfth Street bus. It took almost an hour to get there, so I left home at six in the dark. I never sat down or slowed down all day, and I was going to bed at eight o'clock. I was twenty-one years old, and my friends were calling me every night to go out. It was the third week before I beat the minimum and "$6.00" appeared after my name.

I held my head a little higher. I celebrated by going out with a friend and drinking a couple beers. I got home at ten o'clock and barely made it the next day. After a month on this job, I had not caught the slowest morons among my competitors, but I was gaining on them. The boss came to me and said I had been transferred to another, more complicated machine. I worked there three months.

When the letter came from the Navy saying to report April 3, 1942 to the Naval Barracks at Notre Dame, near South Bend, Indiana, I was overjoyed. I quit my job the next day. To my surprise, two boys on my block that I had known all my life were to report to the Navy the same day, to the same place. Jack Millet and Ward Archer lived next door to each other all their lives and right across the street from me.

We had a week and we played tennis every day. Two nights before we were going to leave, Ward and I had dates and went out on the town. We didn't feel any need to save our money and we had a great time. After we took our dates home, we stopped and had one more drink while we talked about the big adventure we were about to embark on. As we were driving home, Ward Archer looked at his watch and when he saw it was almost two o'clock, he said, "I fear I will be criticized for this nights' work."

When he got home that night, his mother was waiting up for him and he received the criticism he expected. His mother got him up early the next morning and put him to work to punish him. At ten o'clock in the morning, Mrs. Archer called my father at the office. She said, "Ward and David did not get home until after two o'clock this morning. Ward had been drinking and I am sure David had too. Those boys need a lesson and Ward is getting his. I wish you would call Lucille and tell her to get to work on David."

My dad said, "Nell, I appreciate your effort to make men out of our boys. But, I feel it is too late in David's case. He is leaving for the Navy and the war tomorrow and it is too late to straighten him out now."

The Prairie State and the U.S.S. Samuel Chase

I left Kansas City in time to spend two days in Michigan before I reported to the Navy at Notre Dame. I had spent many of my vacations with my Aunt Eva and Uncle Bill in Michigan. Their best friends, JS and Kippie Gray lived in the same town and had a summer house on the same lake. JS and Kippie also had a daughter, Thorne, my age, who was a childhood friend.

The two nights I spent in Michigan I got little sleep. My orders said I should report in on April 3. My Uncle Bill, who drove to me to South Bend, said April 3 lasted until midnight. He said, "There is no use getting there early. Have another beer."

I reported to Notre Dame at five minutes to twelve, midnight, the night of April 3, 1942. They assigned me a bunk in a room with four bunks. The other three bunks were occupied, so I climbed into the empty one and fell asleep.

The next morning, the bugle sounded reveille at five-thirty in the morning. Six hundred apprentice seamen fell in on the parade ground. They were divided into battalions, companies, and platoons, and then they had breakfast. They were assigned lockers and issued uniforms. They reformed into platoons and were given shots. During the short break for lunch, Tom Wallen from West Texas ran back to the room where he had slept to get something he had forgotten. When he walked into the room, he got a jolt when he saw me in my bunk still asleep. He shook me and when I sat up,

He said, "Have you been asleep all this time?"

"All what time? Where is everyone?" I replied.

"Man, we have been organized, assigned platoons, issued lockers, issued uniforms, had shots for everything and been given instructions for everything. Man, you'll never catch up."

I said, "Don't worry about it. I understand it is going to be a long war."

I got dressed, went down and reported my error. I received a tongue-lashing that was right out of the movies and then I caught up. But I had already blown my low profile.

On the morning of the second day, the battalion commander explained that we would be apprentice seamen at Notre Dame for thirty days during which time most of our training would by physical and military. Those who survived the first month would then go to New York and become midshipmen. The course there would be largely academic. Those who survived that course would be commissioned ensigns in the U.S. Naval Services. In the meantime, they had six hundred men here and they could only accommodate five hundred. We were going to run around the track every morning. The first ten men to quit running every morning would be sent home.

"We will tell you when it is time to stop running," he said.

To be in this program, you had to be a college graduate. You had to be single, and you could be up to twenty years old. This was before the day when jogging was popular. Some of these guys had been sitting at a desk for several years without much exercise. I had been working on the nut line at the steel mill. It might not help my IQ, but I was as hard as the nuts and bolts I worked with. There were people falling down and throwing up before I was warmed up. Each day we ran a little farther and at the end of five days the class was the right size. We were apprentice seamen and we wore the uniforms.

At the end of the thirty days, they shipped us to New York. Our quarters in New York were on an old battleship in the Hudson River that had been converted into a school called *The Prairie State. The Prairie State* was tied up to a pier at One-hundred Twenty-Third Street. That was to be our home for the next three months and since our grades had to be in good shape before we could go on a weekend liberty, I seldom left the ship.

When we became midshipmen, they separated those studying to become deck officers from the future engineers. I was the latter. Almost all the engineering midshipmen were graduate engineers. The courses of Steam , Electricity, Damage Control, etc. were much easier for them than they were for me. I had to do my utmost to keep up from the very beginning. I had already flunked out of the Navy Air Corps and I couldn't afford to fail again. We had a test every day in every subject. We ran from one class room to the next. You couldn't study late into the night because everybody had to go to bed at "Taps." Some midshipmen would study after "Taps" by taking flashlights into the "head" and sitting on the toilet in a stall. To correct this, they removed the doors to the stalls.

The only time we could get off *The Prairie State* was on weekends. All our grades for the week had to be passing for us to be eligible for liberty. A list called "the tree" was put up on Saturday at noon. If your name was on that list, you were ineligible to leave *The Prairie State.* The first three weekends, my name was on that list. When the fourth weekend came and my name wasn't on the list, I was ready to see New York. Liberty was from four p.m. on Saturday until four p.m. on Sunday. At ten minutes-to-four on Saturday, I was madly putting my dress blues on when I realized I had very little money. I told two of my friends, "Don't go without me. I will be right back." I ran to the other end of the ship where the deck officers were quartered.

I found Ward Archer at his locker.

I ran up to him and said, "Quick, do you have any money?"

Ward took his billfold out. When he opened it, there was a twenty dollar bill on top. I reached in and took it.

I said, "Thanks. That's just what I need."

Then, I turned and ran back where I came from. Ward's new friends, who lockered on either side of him, watched this operation and one of them said,

"Who was that?"

Ward looked surprised and said, "I don't know. Didn't you know him?"

My first liberty in New York was like a collage: the subways, Times Square, the bar at Astor, the big lighted signs, the crowds of hurrying people, the sex merchants, the uniforms, and me in such a hurry to encounter it all. I did everything too fast and too much. I had a wonderful time. On Sunday, our time was our own until we marched to church in a body at five p.m. We marched to the Riverside Church where the great Harry Emerson Fosdick was the preacher. The first sermon he preached to us made a strong impression on me. He said the war had come at a good time in our lives and it was a great break for us. His message was that since we were all college graduates and all single, we were all candidates for getting married and settling down.

"The sooner you get bored with your job, the sooner you are apt to get married. After you are married and have a family, it is much more difficult to quit the job and maybe the profession itself when you find it is not the way you want to spend your life. You young men are not going to get the opportunity to get married because you are bored with your job: you are going to have an intermission in your life. When the war is over, most of you will still be single. You are going to be older, wiser and more experienced. You may not know just what you want to do for a living, but you are going to know some things you don't want to do. You will make a more mature decision on how you want to spend your life and whom you want to spend it with. most people don't have this opportunity to grow up before they have to make decisions that are hard to turn back on."

As we marched back to *The Prairie State*, I thought Dr. Fosdick made a lot of sense.

I was very aware that there was a teeming life that existed in the neighborhood that surrounded our school. As we marched to and from the Riverside Church or later in the school year, back and forth from Columbia University, I saw the people living in the compact apartments and felt like they lived in a different world than the one in which I lived.

Sometimes I was assigned guard duty on the the pier downriver from The Prairie State.

I was to march back and forth carrying a rifle between two designated spots. My instructions were very explicit: I was to stop fifteen feet short of where the pier touched the land. I was to speak to no one unless I had a challenge to make.

One night while on guard duty, I had been walking about an hour, and a pretty girl about my age came and sat on the end of the pier next to the land. The chalk mark where I turned around was about twelve feet from where she was sitting. The second time I reached that spot and turned around, I realized she was crying. I marched back and forth like a toy solider for three hours while this pretty girl sat there and cried her heart out. I really wanted to stop and ask her what her problem was and could I help her. But as I thought about it, I realized that no matter what her problem was, I couldn't help here. My life was no longer my own. She lived in a different world.

Every week, the office on The Prairie State would receive invitations for midshipmen to attend parties and spend the weekend in one of the nice residential suburbs surrounding New York. There were always more invitations than there were midshipmen who signed up to go. The boys who came from the East Coast were the first ones to jump at these invitations. They realized it was a way to get into the elite suburbs and country clubs where they had never been. The boys from the middle west, like me, had to get their fill of Times Square and the Astor bar before they were willing to spend their weekends with rich girls that might be boring. The process was sped up by the fact that we got paid twenty dollars a month and that didn't last long at the Astor. A weekend at a country club was free.

I had made several good friends among my fellow students. It is easy to make friends when you have so much in common with the people around you. We all had the same hopes and fears. There was a boy from Des Moines, Iowa named Tommy Hoak whose company I enjoyed. When he asked me to sign-up for a party at Pellham, New York for the following weekend, I agreed. We took the train to Pellham along with ten other midshipmen. We were met by station wagons at the station and taken to the house where the party was to be held.

The house where the party was held was large and attractive. There was a swimming pool, a badminton court, and croquet. There was a patio where I could see there was going to be dancing. There was a bar set-up on the yard with a black man in a white coat pouring drinks. A girl touched me on the arm and said,

"Will you be my partner for dinner?"

I said, "I would be delighted."

Then I turned and looked at her. She had a pretty face, but was a little on the heavy side. She said her name was Sophia Troxel. We played croquet and she laughed a lot. When she looked up to see where her croquet ball was going after she hit it, she caught me looking down the front of her low cut dress and laughed even harder.

The band started playing while we were eating the buffet supper. I was amazed at how well Sophia could dance, and she really loved it. When we finally sat down to get our breath, she smiled at me and said, "You know, for a runt of the class, you are a tremendous dancer."

I said, "I'm glad you said that. I have been wanting to say that for a fat girl you have some tremendous moves, and I love dancing with you."

She looked at me and said, "That is a very nice thing to say. I think I am falling in love."

Later in the evening, Tommy Hoak and his girl came by and said I was to share a double bed with Tommy at the Gillette's house. Sophia said, "Not on your life. I've got him and I'm not going to turn him loose. I will take him to my house and bring him over to your house after breakfast." Sophia drove us to her house and it was quite large.

After she parked her car, she asked, "Do you want to go swimming?" I said, "I don't have a swimming suit." Sophia replied, "Too bad." I followed her to the pool and it was a nice one. She said, "You can hang up you clothes in that changing house if you want to." While I stood there with my mouth hanging open, she shed her clothes and made a nice dive into the pool. I hung up my clothes in the dressing room and dove in the pool. I swam down to the other end of the pool where Sophia was. She gave me a big smile, and I said, "You look better without your clothes than you do with them."

She said, "All fat girls do."

Just then the overhead lights at each end of the pool came on. I felt like I was on a stage. Sophia called out," It's me, Sophia. Please turn out the lights." The lights went out. Sophia said, "I think we had better go in before my father comes out and offers you a drink." I said, "I wouldn't care to meet your father under these circumstances."

There was a towel in the changing room, and I dried off and got dressed. We had a sandwich and a glass of milk and Sophia showed me to the guest room. I met her mother and father at breakfast the next morning. There were very friendly. During breakfast, her father said, "I heard you out in the pool last night and I almost came out and offered you a drink, but I was afraid to. Sophia loves to take a skinny dip before she goes to bed, and I was afraid I might catch her without her suit on." Sophia laughed and said, "It is a smart father that knows his own daughter."

Tommy and I went back to Pellham several weekends and I always had a good time.

The school work was hard for me. I was becoming an engineer, something my father had said I would never be. My classmates were almost all graduate engineers and it was a lot easier for them. My hardest course was Electricity and I was just barely getting by. In the last month of the school there was a change in instructors. I was floored when I walked in and saw that the new instructor was a boy from Kansas City who I had known all my life. He was an officer in the Navy and he showed no sign of recognition; but my grades started improving. I don't know whether he had anything to do with it or not.

Two weeks before the end of the school, Tommy and I ended up at Jones Beach on a Saturday afternoon. We met two gorgeous girls that were lying on the beach. We tried to make dates with them for that night. They said they couldn't have dates on Saturday night because they had to work. They were dancers at Billy Rose's Diamond Horseshoe. I had never been there because I couldn't afford it, but I had heard about it. I had heard that the chorus girls were beautiful and everyone was six feet tall. I believed these girls when they said they worked there. They were beautiful, but each was a head taller then I was.

Somebody had nicknamed me "The Deacon" and Tommy had gotten so he called me that. Three days later, over the PA system, came an announcement, "There is a telephone call on the quarter deck for The Deacon of the Prairie State."

I went to the phone booth and gingerly said, "Hello."

A pretty voice said, "This is the girl you met at Jones Beach last Saturday afternoon. You and your friend, Tommy, were trying to make dates with my friend and me. Do you remember?"

"Yes, I remember."

"Would you still like to do that?"

"Yes, sure."

"There is going to be a dance on the *Prairie State* on the night of August the fourth. I don't work that night and I was wondering if you would like for me to be your date."

"I would love for you to be my date."

"Do you remember me? I'm awfully tall."

"I remember you. You are beautiful and tall. I am short. If it doesn't bother you, it won't bother me."

She informed me it was to be a dinner and a dance and told me where and when to meet her. When I met her, I about dropped my teeth. She not only was six feet tall and gorgeous, she had on very high heels and had her hair piled on top of her head. She looked like she was seven feet tall. Everybody looked mighty surprised when we walked in. She stood up straight as an arrow. She had on a low cut dress with big beautiful breasts. She had played this role before and she loved it. She was fun to talk to and had a tremendous sense of humor. When we got up to dance, I felt like I was going to put my chin between her boobs. She was a good dancer, and by standing a couple of inches away from her we could do fine. At one point she said, "Don't get lost down there."

I loved it. Other midshipmen often cut in and danced with my date. When the first one came, my date said, "You'll have to ask my partner." She acted like she hated to have me leave. When the last dance came, the big guy she was dancing with brought her over to me. She said, "I thought we should dance this last dance together." She wouldn't let anyone else cut in.

The whole evening was a great success.

I graduated the next day. I received my commission as an ensign in the United States Navy and took my orders to report to the Amphibious Force in Norfolk after a five-day leave. Quite a few of the graduates were assigned to the Amphibious Force and most of them were greatly disappointed. They expected to be assigned to a battleship, a cruiser, or at least a destroyer. We were the first class to have anyone assigned to the Amphibs and no one knew much about it except that it was supposed to be terribly dangerous. I was so glad to graduate and get my commission, I didn't care where I was assigned.

My orders were to report aboard the *USS Samuel Chase* on August 11th at Norfolk. I arrived the night before and spent the night in the Monticello Hotel. The next morning I went to the restaurant across the street for breakfast. There was an ensign, with a uniform that looked as new as mine, sitting alone so I asked him if I could join him. He was Bill Fitzgerald from Utica, New York. His orders were the same as mine. When we ordered breakfast, Fitzgerald ordered a bowl of cornflakes and a bottle of beer. While we were waiting for our order, Bill told me he was a school teacher. He intended to make school teaching his career. He had graduated from college the year before. Then waitress brought our breakfast. To the complete amazement of the waitress and myself, Fitzgerald, without missing a beat in the conversation, poured the beer on his cornflakes. Then he took his spoon and began to eat it.

He told me he was an only child. His mother was a school teacher and he couldn't remember his father. He said that being the son of a school teacher, he was very aware that a teacher had a certain image to maintain, and he was prepared to do this. He said he looked forward to owning a house in the suburbs and spending the weekends mowing the yard and washing the car. And since he was going to spend the rest of his life living like this he was going to use the period of his life in the Navy to raise all the hell he could. All of this came out while he was eating cornflakes with beer. He sounded like a fun guy to be with.

The day I reported aboard the *USS Samuel Chase,* about sixty other new ensigns reported aboard. I saluted the colors and said, "Request permission to come aboard," just as I had been trained on *The Prairie State*. The officer of the deck said, "If you are an engineering officer, go to the fantail and report to Lieutenant Kouri. If you are a deck officer go forward and report to Lieutenant Jones." I made a quick decision and went forward to find Lt. Jones. My commission said I was an engineer, but I knew better. It took the Navy two years to find out I had made the switch and by that time it was too late.

I thought the *USS Samuel Chase* was going to Africa and we would make an amphibious landing where the war was going on. That turned out not to be the case. We spent a month cruising around Chesapeake Bay waiting for the first amphibious base to be built at Solomon, Maryland. We were also waiting for the first LCTs to be built. An LCT is a Landing Craft-Tank one hundred and five feet long, is run by three two-hundred and twenty-five horsepower diesel engines and has a crew of ten enlisted men and one officer. It is designed to carry tanks from an attack transport to the beach. Or, at least, that is what they told us while we were on the *Samuel Chase.* During that month, I had one ride on an LCT. At the end of a month, we had a weekend of liberty at Virginia Beach, where Bill Fitzgerald and I met some girls and had a wonderful time.

We next spent ten days at the new amphibious base in Solomon, Maryland. During this ten days, we had two instructional periods on how to dock an LCT. One time, I actually got to try it. Then we move to an amphibious base under construction at Little Creek, ten or fifteen miles out of Norfolk.

My father had a college buddy from Princeton named Mac McPherin and he had stayed in touch ever since he graduated in 1910. Mac McPherin owned a business in Norfolk. Mac had two lovely daughters. Mr. McPherin treated me like a long-lost son, and his wife and daughters couldn't have been friendlier. Lyba McPherin, the older of the two daughters, was twenty-two. She had her own car and her family belonged to a nice club. Norfolk had been a Navy-base town for a long time, so the long-time citizens of Norfolk had become disillusioned and prejudiced against anybody in a sailor suit. The old story was that the barber shops had signs that said "No dogs or sailors allowed." Consequently, the access I had to home cooking and hospitality through the McPherins was even more valuable. There were very few LCT officers who had any way of getting a date with a nice girl except through me. Lyba and her mother made my stay there very pleasant.

The tenth of October, thirty LCT officers and three hundred enlisted men were quickly and quietly loaded aboard a train and departed Norfolk. It was a regular passenger train with no one on it but us and the train crew. We had regular Pullman cars in which the black porter came through at night and made up our berths. We had dining cars with regular black dining-car waiters. We also had a commanding officer. Lt. Commander Yeager, it was rumored, who had been the commanding officer of a girls camp in civilian life. Lt. Commander Yeager knew we were going to San Francisco and he brought his wife along for the trip. The enlisted men were all apprentice seamen and the vast majority of them were seventeen years old. They were not the cream of their high school classes but were a rowdy bunch. Lt. Commander Yeager's background had not prepared him to deal with these three hundred seventeen-year-olds.

On the second day, the waiters and cooks quit. Twice a day the conductor would pick a town that had the capacity to feed our three hundred-thirty men and one woman. He would wire ahead and ask them if they would feed us. The train would stop and we would march our three hundred-man party to the restaurant.

If we went too long without eating, the sailors would get abusive. None of the enlisted men had been assigned to any of the officers, and keeping any semblance of order seemed to be no one's job, except Lt. Commander Yeager.

One day we traveled all morning without stopping. We were down near the Mexican border and there was no town capable of feeding our large party. In the afternoon we stopped and they fed us in five nightclubs. In the nightclub I ate in, they put on a floor show. Everyone loved it. When we marched back to the train, the local citizens lined the sidewalks and waved. Lt. Commander Yeager and his wife marched out in front. It made a great parade.

San Francisco Adventures

At the end of a week we arrived in San Francisco and were bussed to a barracks at Treasure Island. The officers shared a barracks with the officers of a British ship that had been sunk. They seemed like a subdued lot that were not particularly interested in socializing with a group of American officers in new uniforms.

Each of the LCT officers, including me, was assigned ten enlisted men to be our crew. I learned that of the ten men, eight of them were only seventeen years old. One, Frank Gorski, was eighteen and Arden Heyd was twenty-five. Gorski was to be the bosun's mate, which meant he was to be my right-hand man. Ralph Goforth was going to be the cook, and York and Peterson were to be in charge of the engines because they were striking for motor machinist mates. The LCT's started arriving and were assigned to crews.

We were told that the LCT's were badly needed in the South Pacific because there were no docks or piers to unload the supply ships. The LCT had a big ramp for a bow. The landing craft was designed to be run up on the beach and the ramp lowered. It was just what they needed in the Pacific. How to transport them was the problem. First they tried towing one but the cable broke when they tried to pick up speed. The war would be over before we could get there. In the end, they took the LCT apart and loaded it on the deck of a large cargo ship. The LCT was built in three sections that would float separately. It was bolted together with hundreds of bolts.

On November 4, 1942 I received orders from the Bureau of Personnel saying I was the officer in charge of LCT 324. Lt. Commander Yeager handed me the orders and told me where the ship was. I was to get it immediately and tie it up in the slip between Pier 40 and 42. I rounded up my ten men and went after it.

It was new, and it was gigantic. I told York to give me time to get up to the pilot house and then start the engines. I stood on the bridge and gave orders to the helmsman and the throttle man through the little windows into the pilot house. Griffith was the helmsman and Sneigouski was the throttle man. Gorski was in charge of the men handling the lines.

We got her underway and headed out into the big bay with no problems, but when we got down to Pier 40 and started to turn in I found we were going the same direction as the tide and we sailed right on past it. We turned around, which was educational in itself, and started back. The second time, I went out in the bay where I could get a straight shot at the slip I wanted in. By the time we got to the entrance of the slip, the tide and the wind had carried us past it. That first day, it took me four tries to get the LCT 324 into the slip where it belonged. By the time I did it, I had bounced off of both Pier 40 and Pier 42 and acquired an audience.

The next two days were spent opening the boxes of supplies for the new boat, trying to figure out what they were and putting them away. There were a lot of things I figured we would never use. There were quite a few things we couldn't identify. I put the books on navigation and the forty-five automatic pistol in my quarters. Goforth put the pots and pans and dishes in the galley. I appointed a working party to draw supplies so we could start cooking and eating. Suddenly we were an independent unit and immediately everyone asked if they could go on liberty. We were tied up right on the Embarcadero at the foot of Market Street. The "dens of iniquity" seemed very handy. I divided the crew in half and said half could go each night. They were raring to go. Most of those who went got drunk and were sick the next day. Being sick the next day was almost like a badge of honor and they were proud of it, but they were not very alert in helping me handle the boat.

Every morning the port director would give us a job to do for that day. We would go someplace in the San Francisco Bay area and pick up cargo that was to be delivered to some other location in the bay area. They were getting some good use out of the LCTs while we were waiting orders to the South

Pacific and the work gave me and some other skippers some practice and experience which was badly needed. With such a strong tide and so much traffic, it was a tough place to learn. Fortunately, the pilings and the piers were sturdy and strong, as was the LCT. Most of the criticism came when I would hit another ship. There were ships loading and waiting to be loaded everywhere. I would come into a slip to tie up a little too fast as the tide was carrying me past the entrance. Once, I banked off the side of a merchant ship that was loading on the other side of the slip. When I often found myself on a collision course with the Oakland ferry, I would back down because I knew he wouldn't. But most of the other local craft kept as far away from me as they could. It was reported that seven different outfits were suing the Navy for things we had run into.

The development of the crew during these five months was an interesting thing to watch. They were growing up and they were loving it. Red Gothardt was a perfect example. Red was seventeen and a big strong boy. His parents had had to sign the papers for Red to join the Navy because he was under age. Red turned eighteen during those five months and he got an education in the dives of San Francisco that he would never have gotten in his hometown of Letonia, Ohio. He was pretty proud when he came back to the LCT one night with a big tree tattooed on his back. I had to admit I had never seen a tree like that on anybody. Ralph Goforth, our cook, was the same age as Red and he was jealous of Red's tattoo. Goforth got a heart with a dagger sticking through it and underneath the word "Mother." When almost everyone had a tattoo, Red got a second one.

These young men went out every other night looking for adventure and they usually found it in some form. On a perfect night, they would get drunk, have a fight, and go to bed with a girl. They seldom got all three. The only member of the crew that did not join in this activity was twenty-seven-year old Arden Heyd. He came from a small farm town in northern Michigan. He was striking for gunner's mate, he could do almost anything and was very cooperative. I was working my head off every day and going to bed exhausted every night. I was glad to have Ardie Heyd with a clear head ready to help me in the morning while half the crew were still getting their heads straightened out.

One morning, Goforth and Gothardt appeared to have lost a fight with some Marines the night before. They asked Ardie Heyd to come and help them on their next liberty. He finally agreed to do it. When they came back to the LCT they had won the battle with the Marines and had gotten so drunk that Ardie Heyd was still drunk the next day. I felt I had the full load with nobody helping me. After a sleepless night, I got up early in the morning and walked out to the end of the pier where there was a public phone booth and called my father in Kansas City. I told him the whole rotten story and asked his advice.

He said, "Have you been going ashore and having fun, Dave?"

I said, "No. I have too much responsibility not to be sharp the first thing in the morning."

My dad said, "I think you would find if you failed to get up some morning that somebody else in the crew would. You aren't giving those fellows a chance to show what they can do. My suggestion to you is that you find another skipper that wants to go out and see the town. You tell the crew before you go that they should be ready to take over in the morning in case you don't get up. I think you will be pleasantly surprised at how well the work keeps on going without you."

San Francisco was not an open city of sin in 1942. There were, of course, many bars and night clubs in which young men wearing a naval officer's uniform were most welcome. There were many floor shows and entertainers. It was easy to get drunk, beat up and robbed. But if you wanted to get in serious trouble, you had to work at it. Fortunately for me, I had two good friends who were a year or two older than I and much more sophisticated in the ways of the city at night. Harvey Shuler and Bob Willits invited me to go to the La Fiesta Night Club with them. It was better than the places I had found on my own. They had a floor show with a chorus line of attractive girls dancing in unison in good-looking outfits. Somehow, Willits established communication with them and when the night club closed at two a.m. we had dates to take three of them to supper. I would never have gotten this done by myself. I thought supper at two-thirty in the morning would be scrambled eggs, but I was wrong. This was their big meal of the day, and they ate steaks. That was one thing about San Francisco: you could order a big dinner at any hour. We met several girls and enjoyed more than one evening watching the show and going out afterwards.

I went to a dance one night that was put on by the Junior League in San Francisco. It was for lonely Naval officers just like me. The setting and the food were fine but the girls weren't very pretty and I didn't seem to be in the mood. I was standing over at the side eating sandwiches when the girl who I had picked out as the prettiest one there came over and asked me to dance. She said, "We can't have a successful party if you just stand around and eat." We talked and danced until some guy cut in and I went back to being sullen again. After a while she came back and asked me to dance again. This time, she said, "The party is almost over. When it is, I have arranged for us to go with another couple that have a car to a little restaurant where they have fresh oysters. Do you like oysters?"

"Yes, I like oysters, but I am not a good guy to take because I don't have any money." The girl, whose name was Frances Hubbard, said, "Why not? Don't you live on the ship in the harbor?"

"Yes."

"Then your board and room are furnished. You got paid less than a week ago. What did you do with your money? Do you send it home in an allotment?"

"No, I don't send it anywhere. I spent it."

"Are you married? Do you support your mother?"

"You are getting very nosy, but the truth is I am a wastrel and I have spent that good money the Navy gave me."

She said, "Well, I guess I can carry you until next payday, and then I will take charge of your paycheck."

Frances did just what she said she was going to do and from then on I never ran out of money. She would spend my last dollar the day before I got paid. She bought tickets two and three weeks ahead of time for everything that was coming to town. She planned trips to California's redwood forest and places of interest that I would never have dreamt of going. I paid for everything but with no bars or nightclubs my money went a lot farther. We rode streetcars everywhere we went and I stopped paying for taxis.

Frances was pretty, enthusiastic and seemed to think that I was just what she had in mind. I had never had anyone plan my social life and I enjoyed it. She lived in a small apartment near the Golden Gate Park with her mother and her mother always seemed to be in it when I brought Frances home. Some nights, we would sit on the steps in the hall to talk and not disturb her mother. I found she had read all the same books I had. She liked the same poems.

Frances had gone two years to school at the University of California at Berkeley. She had belonged to a sorority there and we went to several functions there, including a sorority dance. I looked up the Phi Gamma Delta fraternity house there, went in and introduced myself. They gave me a warm welcome and invited me to bring Frances to their dance.

In spite of the parties and pretty girls, the war was still going on and we were being readied to deploy. One by one, the LCTs were being taken apart and loaded aboard cargo ships and sent to the war zone in the South Pacific. I kept thinking I would go next week. Frances was buying tickets to plays that were three weeks away. I kept saying, "This may be our last night." She acted like I was going to be there forever.

In the meantime, I was fighting the battle of San Francisco Bay every day. We would get orders from the port director's office every morning to pick up cargo at some point in the bay area and carry it to some other point. I was getting excellent experience in boat handling and so was the crew. One morning, I backed over the big five-inch manila hawser and got it firmly wrapped around the port screw. That means I backed over the big rope we tie the boat up with and got it badly tangled in the left-hand propeller. I swam down to look at it and discovered that each of the three propellers was in a hollowed-out recess like the top of a tunnel. They were not located right at the stern of the ship like the toy boat in my bathtub. The propellers were about three feet forward of the transom at the extreme end of the ship. The hull of the LCT was made up of tanks that could be used for the storage of fuel oil, water, ballast or whatever. There were holes to pump into or out of every tank. I decided to pump everything out of the stern tanks and to fill all the bow tanks with the hope of getting the stern up in the air high enough for me to cut the rope out of the propeller. I had already determined when I had swum under the ship that the big manila line was stretched so tight and so many times around the shaft that it was hard as concrete. The main thing I wanted to avoid was having the Navy find out that I had rendered my boat inoperable by doing the land-lubberly thing anyone could do — namely, backing over my own hawser. After I had the forward tanks full and the stern tanks empty, I found that although it tipped the boat forward, the stern was not quite out of the water. I took a big hunting knife and swam under the stern to the left propeller. I found the tunnel the propeller was in was about halfway out of the water. I could stick my head against the bottom of the ship and breathe captured air while I worked on the frozen line. I had a place to work, but the hunting knife didn't do any good at all. I swam back out under the stern and called for a hacksaw. About half the crew was standing on the rear deck looking for a report. I swam back and tried the hacksaw, but I found I couldn't get to it all. I ended up sitting on one blade of the propeller with my head pressed against the bottom of the ship while I used a hammer and chisel to cut the last two layers of hard, wet manila line. I was in this position when someone in the engine room started the right hand engine. We were securely tied to the pier and they were doing a little testing. One of the onlookers on the stern saw the wake come out of the starboard engine and made a dash for the engine room. The engine was immediately stopped. But by then, I was so terrified that the propeller I was draped around was going to start turning that I was almost out of my mind. I was beating on the bottom of the ship with my bare hands yelling, "Don't start the motor. I am down here." I got the rest of the hawser off of the propeller shaft. I then swore the crew to secrecy. I said they would not only laugh us off the waterfront, they would probably relieve me of my command.

About a week later, the crew was awakened in the middle of the night by the noise of my beating on the metal bulkhead beside my bunk with my bare fists. I was screaming, "Don't start the engine! I am down here. Don't start the engine!" I had this nightmare for weeks.

On to the Pacific

I received orders to remove the hundreds of bolts that held the three water-tight sections of my ship together in preparation for having them lifted aboard a large ocean-going freighter. Our date of departure was April 23rd, 1943. After I bought a case of Scotch and put it under my bunk, I had twenty dollars left. The orders read that my crew and I were to be on board the freighter by 01800 hours, six o'clock in the evening.

Frances Hubbard didn't get off work until five o'clock and I hadn't had a chance to say goodbye to her. We went to a very nice bar close to the waterfront where we had a couple of drinks and said very romantic things to each other. We took a cab to the Pier, I gave the driver my last dollar. Frances kissed me goodbye and I went up the gangway and prepared to leave the mainland.

It was a dark night when we sailed under the Golden Gate Bridge and headed west across the Pacific. I was starting on a great adventure and I loved the idea. The six months I had spent carrying cargo around San Francisco harbor had made me feel very capable of handling my LCT. I had learned how to get the work out of my crew, and I felt we were ready for whatever came next. Still, my trips in San Francisco harbor had not prepared me for the groundswells off the coast of California. When I hit the sack that night, I was dead tired, had no money, and nothing in my stomach.

Aboard the freighter, my crew slept in their own bunks in the LCT. They used the bathroom and showers of the freighter. I shared a stateroom with a Navy ensign named Blain who was the only other passenger on the freighter. I woke up the next morning feeling fine but empty. In the dining room the steward's mate handed me a menu where you put an "x" in each box to show what you wanted in each course. I had never had this opportunity before, and I loved it. After I had a long look at the ocean going by, I went to see how my crew was getting along. I found several of them tying the big stern anchor of the LCT to the anchor braces. They said that every time the ship rolled during the night, our stern anchor banged against the stern of the LCT and kept them awake. I tried to think of things or projects for them to do. They didn't have any responsibilities, and neither did I.

It took us thirty-one days to reach Noumea, New Caledonia, and we saw no land or ships during that time. I played poker almost every night, and I almost always won. I had one hundred forty-nine dollars when they unloaded my LCT in Noumea. That served as my stake, and I never drew a paycheck while I was overseas.

After they unloaded the three waterproof sections of my LCT in Noumea Harbor, our first job was to bolt them back together. It was a lot of bolts to tighten, but we had ten strong young men who hadn't had anything to do for thirty-one days, and they really worked at it. We had tied up next to another LCT because we couldn't drop our anchor. It was still tied to the anchor braces on the stern. The temperature was well over a hundred degrees, and we were working inside these steel sections of the hull where there was no ventilation. When we finished the job, we felt that we had earned a rest. The skipper of the LCT we were tied up next to was my old friend, Bill Fitzgerald, from Virginia Beach. He had advised us and watched us bolt the sections together. When we finished, he said he had a reward for me. Before he left San Francisco, he had bought a case of beer and put it under his bunk.

There was no refrigeration of any kind on an LCT. I had never drunk warm beer before. We sat there in that tropical sun and drank several bottles of that warm beer. Bill and I started thinking of the important things we had to do. He was the captain of his own ship with duties to perform.

I remembered that our anchor was still secured to the stern, and I went to the anchor winch and tried to drop it. The lines securing it to the anchor braces held it and it wouldn't fall. I climbed over the stern and tried to untie the lines holding it. The weight of the big anchor was too much of a strain on the lines and I couldn't untie them. I went to my cabin and got the marine hunting knife the Navy had issued me. I climbed over the stern and down the anchor. By hanging onto the anchor brace with my left arm, I could reach the line that was pulled tight and keeping the anchor from falling. The line was a heavy one, but stretched tight I was able to cut through it with my sharp knife. When the two thousand pound anchor fell, it fortunately missed my head, but it grazed my left arm that was holding me on the brace and the anchor and I fell into the bay.

Several members of the crew were watching me perform this operation and they thought the anchor had hit me in the head. There was a lot of excitement as they assisted me back aboard my ship. One of the crew called Captain Fitzgerald and he took over. He announced that he would rush me to the hospital ship. I said that as far as I could tell there wasn't anything wrong with me. He said, "You never can tell." Furthermore, the day before, he had been issued a rubber boat with an outboard motor with instructions that it should only be used in an emergency. He had been waiting for an emergency just like this.

The harbor at Noumea is large. It was about three miles from where we were anchored to where the *USS Solace,* the Navy's hospital ship, was anchored. We arrived there without incident, and Fitzgerald deposited me on the little metal platform at the foot of the ladder up the side of the *Solace.* The "ladder" is a regular metal stairway going up the side of this big ship. At the top to the ladder is an area called the quarterdeck, where the officer of the day presides. This OD was a heavyset older man who looked like he didn't approve of my get-up. I had on Navy blue dungarees and an officer's hat. The dungarees are work clothing normally worn by enlisted men. I saluted, requested permission to come aboard and explained my problem. He sent a messenger to conduct me. The *Solace* is a gigantic floating hospital. They x-rayed me and sure enough, my arm was broken. Also, the four fingers of my left hand were broken. When they finished with me, I had a large cast that included my hand and extended almost to my elbow. Then, I went to look for Fitzgerald and my ride back to my ship.

I found him, sleeping in the rubber boat off side of the Solace. He was hard to awaken, and had trouble getting the motor started, but finally came around and I joined him in the boat. The nap that Fitzgerald had had in the sun while he was waiting for me, coupled with all the beer he had drunk and the exercise of starting the motor, had really made him perspire. He was soaking wet and he said, "I have to have something to drink." We were out in the middle of the big bay and a destroyer entering the bay looked like it was on a collision course with us. Suddenly, Fitzgerald jumped up and began wildly waving his arms. He had shut our motor off and we sat dead in the water, bobbing around right in the destroyer's way. Fitz was still waving his arms.

I said, "What in the world are you doing?"

Fitz said, "I want to get a drink."

The destroyer slowed down and then backed down. It looked gigantic from our rubber boat. A head came over the side and said, "What's the trouble down there?"

Fitz said, "We're survivors. We need emergency supplies. We need a couple gallons of gas and a pitcher of lemonade."

I could see a conference going on on their bridge and in a minute a line was lowered over the side with a pitcher of lemonade tied to it. The head came back and said, "Tie your gas can to the line and I will fill it up for you." We got our can back and continued our journey back to our ships.

The next day, Fitzgerald and I reported to the Navy port director and were told to fill our fresh water tanks, our diesel tanks and make sure we had at least thirty days' supply of food. The PD said we would be attached to the next convoy going north. While I was waiting to take on fresh water, I tied up next to a New Zealand corvette [a small, armed war ship]. We had nothing but a magnetic compass on our LCT to navigate with, and it hadn't been compensated since we took the LCT apart and put it back together. I checked against the gyro compass on the corvette. There was twenty-three degrees difference when we were tied up side by side. I told the captain of the corvette, and he thought I should not get out of sight of land. He was so friendly, I asked him about the ration of rum which I had heard the English Navy still had. Did this apply to the ships of New Zealand as well? By all means. He explained some of the rules. An enlisted man who was non-rated with a certain grade had to have his rum cut with water. Once he became rated with a certain grade he could drink it neat. While he was explaining it to me, he called a sailor over and gave some instruction. The sailor came back with a tray with two water glasses full of rum.

"I thought you might like to try our rum so you know what we are talking about."

We were sitting in deck chairs in the boiling sun, and it was well over a hundred degrees. We clinked glasses and the captain said, "Here's to our friendship." To my horror, he downed the whole water glass full of rum. I downed mine, too. I asked if he had to account for the rum, and he said there was allowable percentage for shrinkage. I then went back to my LCT, got in my bunk, and waited for the feeling to pass. I didn't want to cut any more anchors loose.

When the port director told us we would be sailing to Tulagi with one stop at Espiritu Santo, a distance of about fourteen hundred miles, I asked him for a set of charts. He said they couldn't afford to give us one. They didn't have enough. Anyway, he said, you will be in convoy.

"Just follow the ship ahead of you."

The only chart I had was of the whole Pacific Ocean. Noumea and Tulagi were very close together.

On the night before we were to leave, I had a final warm beer with Fitzgerald and returned to the LCT 324 in my own rubber boat. I was sitting on my bunk just starting to untie my Navy-issue high top shoes when one of the crew ran into me and said, "Goforth just fell off the bow." I jumped up and ran for the bow. I knew Goforth couldn't swim. There was only one other person on the ship that could swim besides me and it sure wasn't Goforth. I climbed up on the bow deck, which is about ten feet above the water. There were three of the crew standing there pointing.

"There he is. There he is."

There was bright moonlight and I could see the white of his t-shirt. I dived for him. When I came up and tried to grab Goforth, for the first time I remembered the cast on my arm. He was either unconscious or almost, because he didn't give me any help or any resistance at all. I got my left elbow under his left armpit and started swimming toward the bow of the LCT. I yelled for the men on the bow deck to throw me a line. One of them called back and said there was already a line hanging against the side of the bow. That ten foot wall of steel was in the shadow and I couldn't see the line. They said it was right below them. I swam to it pulling Goforth. It was quite dark in the shadow, and I was amazed to find when I got there that there was another sailor in the water hanging on the line. The other sailor was Pagliaro, and although Goforth was an average-sized eighteen-year-old, Pagliaro was a six foot eighteen-year-old.

Pagliaro said, "Thank God, you've come."

And with that, he turned loose of the line and threw both arms around my neck. All three of us went under and after we got so far down, Pagliaro turned loose of me and fought his way back up to the line. When Goforth and I came back up, I remained out of Pagliaro's reach. I reasoned with him.

"Tony, let me hold onto the rope, too. Just relax. Don't grab me when I take hold of the rope. I have Goforth here and everything is going to be all right if we don't panic."

He let me take hold of the rope, then he locked his legs around my middle. I called to the sailors on the bow deck, "Lower the ramp. Lower the ramp."

It seemed to me they were an awful long time in lowering that ramp. The truth is we had lowered it very few times, and their captain wasn't there to tell them how. When I finally heard the ramp come down, I said, "Tony, if you will turn loose of me, I will swim Goforth over to the ramp and then I will come back for you." He didn't give in easily, but as I reassured him, he gradually relaxed. When his legs slipped away from my middle, I headed for the ramp with Goforth. It was about thirty feet of water around there, and the crew was waiting to lift him out. I went back after Tony and although he was harder to work with than Goforth, we finally made it. When I climbed out on the ramp, exhausted, I was greeted by the news, "Goforth is dead."

I said, "Lay him on his side and pump the water out of him. Griffith, you call the hospital ship and tell them to come and get him."

These were the days before CPR, and I couldn't give Goforth artificial respiration because of my hand. But the crew took turns pumping on him. They got a lot of water out of him, but there was no sign of life. Finally, he began to have convulsions. Then, some blood came out of his mouth and he began to gasp and then breathe. By the time the hospital ship got there, he was breathing pretty evenly, but he had not regained consciousness. They took him back to the *USS Solace*, where they put him in an oxygen tent. He caught up with us about six weeks later.

I should have gone to the hospital ship with Goforth and gotten a new cast, but I didn't think of it. By morning, I realized that my cast was beyond salvaging. The Goforth swim had ruined it. There was no time to do anything about it, as the convoy was leaving. The great adventure was about to begin. Arden Heyd cut the cast off my arm and cut a board that ran from my elbow to the end of my fingers. Then he taped my arm and fingers flat to the board. It wasn't perfect, but it was better then missing the convoy. My crew was so anxious to get to where the war was, I couldn't hold them up.

We followed the convoy out of the harbor that morning, and by the end of the first two hours, I knew it was going to be a bad deal. An LCT is one hundred and five feet long with a very shallow draft and a flat bottom. It is designed for landing on a sand beach. In a flat sea it will run eight to ten miles an hour. In an average rough sea with the wind blowing in the wrong direction, it will run three to five miles per hour. We were experts in San Francisco Bay, but we had never had our LCT in the open sea. From the very beginning, we were falling behind. At the end of the first hour, we had received two messages from the destroyer on the right flank of the column: "Increase speed." We were running our engines wide open, and it was a very rough ride. Our bow would go up in the air and come completely out of the water. When it came down, it would smack the water with a loud "bam." The spray was so thick that you got soaked when you stood on the open bridge. When you steered from the wheelhouse, you could hardly see through the slits in the armor plate. The larger ships felt that they were sitting ducks for the Japanese submarines at this slow speed. They were getting farther and farther ahead of us.

When I went below to get a cup of coffee, I was shocked at the condition of the galley. The food and dishes had fallen out of the cabinets and were all over. The crew were either in their bunks or sitting around their lunch counter, seasick. I was not sick. I was too worried to get sick. I kept thinking of the only big chart that we had and remembering the twenty-three degrees difference between our compass and the one on the New Zealand corvette. The other LCT in the convoy was on our port side and by afternoon, even the other LCT was leaving us behind. When supper time came, the cook was too sick to cook. Gorski opened a can of Spam, but only about three of us ate anything. When it began to get dark, I realized that there would be no lights to follow. There was strict radio silence and we could barely see the other ships in the daylight. All we could do when it got dark was follow the compass heading we were on. I had divided the crew into three watches with each watch serving four hours on and eight off. That meant that there were at least three of us up there all the time. I had been up on the bridge all day, and I finally reluctantly climbed in my bunk with all my clothes on. I didn't need the drone of the motors to put me to sleep.

When I woke up, it was daylight and I raced to the bridge. Griffith was at the wheel. He was the only official helmsman we had, as he was striking for quartermaster. There wasn't a ship in sight.

"Where is everybody?"

"The LCT is off the port bow, right over there. You can barely see it through the binoculars."

The sea was a little calmer than it had been the day before, but it was still hard to hold the binoculars steady. When our deck went up in the air, I could barely see the speck on the horizon. They were evidently steering a course a little to the west of our course. I changed our course five degrees to the left. Somebody prepared some dehydrated eggs, but it wasn't the cook: he was too sick. We weren't bouncing as bad as the first day, and the spray didn't drive me into the pilot house. I thought I was safer there in the fresh air than in the stale air of the crew quarters and galley. The crew was still sick. Even the guy that cooked the eggs didn't eat them.

During the morning, another ship appeared on the horizon directly ahead of us. It turned out to be the destroyer, and it had come back close enough to blink us a signal. Whenever we got a signal, it took the whole crew to figure it out. Our signalman striker was learning to read the dots and dashes, as was everyone else. The signal was, "Maintain course. Stay with other LCT." This me feel a lot better because it sounded like we were on the right course. I am sure he sent the same signal to the other LCT, and we began to close the distance between us.

I started down to my room to get the book I had bought in San Francisco called *Navigation Made Easy*. I was beginning to think I was going to need it. When I passed through the crews' quarters, I decided it was more important to do something here. I asked Arden Heyd to help me clean up the galley. No one had done any dishes for two days. There were plates of half-eaten food everywhere. There were broken dishes and cans of food scattered. Goforth had been our cook and he was a poor one, but when he had been transferred to the hospital ship, they gave us a new cook named Van Arsdale. He looked like he was going to do better than Goforth, but so far on this trip, his stomach had not let him spend much time in the galley. When Griffith saw Heyd and me cleaning up the mess, he pitched in and helped. It is hard to do dishes with your left hand tied to a board.

In the afternoon, the sun came out and we arrived at Espiritu Santo. When we wound our way around the buoys marking the mine field into this beautiful harbor, we were a proud and humble team. The most frequently asked question was, "How long do we get to stay here?"

Our convoy had had enough of us, and when we left Buttons, which was the Navy name for Espiritu Santo, we had new friends to sail with. The trip from there to Tulagi was about the same distance, but it wasn't as rough. When I wasn't on the bridge, I was reading the book on navigation. Going through midshipman school as an engineer, I had studied no navigation. When daylight would finally come and I could see no other ship on the horizon, I would go down and start reading that navigation book. When we arrived at Tulagi, there was an air raid going on. We were thrilled. We had made it to the war. I went ashore and reported in. The Navy captain I reported to said, "Good. We need you badly."

Letters to the Homefront

David Hawley wrote regular letters home to his parents, his sister Harriett, brother George, cousin Ann, aunts and uncles. He had an occasional correspondence with his childhood friend, Thorne Gray. These letters not only tell the story of David's feelings throughout his many wartime experiences, but paint a good picture of the South Pacific during World War II.

June 8th, 1943

Dear Mother and Dad:

I have arrived at my ultimate destination, only to be told to be ready in a few days to move on. If I keep moving on the Japs will have to move over or there won't be any room for me.

Dorothy Lamour and Bob Hope have painted a very deceitful picture of this part of the world.

I have been working like a dog. Last night I was so tired I could hardly sleep. Today was a little easier as I am getting more organized every day. I have run into several of my old friends. Today I ran into Bud Jones. He was my old commanding officer who I liked so much. He is in command of the base out of which I will be operating. However, I don't think I will be seeing him very often. He had had malaria and lost about forty pounds. I hardly recognized him.

I can't tell you about the scenery, but it is just like a story book. It would cost a million dollars to take a trip like this, and if I did, I would just be a passenger and not the captain of my own ship. I am out here where history is being made and I am proud to be a part of it. Six months ago people laughed at our barges. Now the big shots say "I don't know what we would do without them."

Dave

June 19, 1943

Dear Aunt Eva and Uncle Bill:

It has been a long time since I have written you and a great deal has happened to me. I left the United States on April 23rd, and in less than two months, I have covered a lot of ground — or should I say a lot of water.

As I wrote Mother and Dad, they broke my boat up into three pieces to bring it across. When we got here I had to put it together myself. We had never tried it, but were successful. I thought I was at the fighting front then. Three days later I shoved off to go to the advanced base, which was a distance of twelve hundred miles. I made this trip under my own power. When I got there I decided I must be at the most advanced base. I thought this must be Tokyo. Anyhow, they weren't kidding when they said this base was advanced. I am considering suggesting to the admiral that we move it back a little.

Supplies of any kind are hard to get out here, and every outfit is working for themselves. Our boats have done a wonderful job out here, and because of it, I am treated very well wherever I go. I am very independent, but have to work hard. My boat is either loading, unloading, or underway twenty-four hours a day. My greatest worry is getting sick. The weather and water are not conducive to good health. This week the whole crew, including me, has a touch of dysentery, which makes our trips to the washroom very frequent. Some of the boats which have been out here longer than I, have had a great deal of malaria. Our boss, Uncle Bud, has had the malaria four times. However, they all seem to live through it.

Some mornings we have to sweep the shrapnel off our decks that has fallen on them the night before. A Fourth of July celebration will never impress me again. Some nights, you can read a book on the deck from the lights in the sky. Some of the soldiers around here have been killed by being hit on the head with coconuts when they were on the beach. That would be a very unromantic way to die.

There is no beer up here. The only thing the men can find to drink is what they call "PT juice." They make it out of grain alcohol and grapefruit juice. They get the alcohol out of the torpedoes from the PT boats. I haven't tried it, but I heard some boys on the beach mixing a batch of it the other night. It caught fire from one of the boy's cigarettes, and burnt down the grass shack in which they were mixing it.

Love, Dave

June 20, 1943

Dear Mother and Dad,

I haven't been paid since I left the States, and I see no indication of it in the near future. But it doesn't bother me, as there is no place to spend any money. Everything out here of value is traded — usually for food; money has no value. Such things as fresh meat, canned fruit juice, and fresh fruit cannot be bought with money. But if you have a motor part that they need, or a Jap hunting knife, or a good sun helmet or sun goggles, you might talk business. I bought the most expensive pair of sunglasses in San Francisco before I left and they have proven very helpful. Of course, whiskey is the high card when it comes to trading.

I realize now that people in the States eat a lot more than they need, simply from habit. You can learn to get along on a lot less. We simply don't have that much food out here. When they said, "An army travels on its stomach", they were dead right. Of course, we are the pirates of the South Seas and eat better than most. We steal food along with everything else, but there is nothing they can do about it, as we are the lifeline to the most advanced bases.

The uniforms we wear are very informal; most of the men wear shorts and shoes. It is almost impossible to tell what a man's rank is by his uniform. In the daytime, we wear sun helmets. I have a two-way radio on my boat, and in the evenings I listen to the news broadcasts from San Francisco. Then I turn the dial and listen to the news broadcasts from Tokyo. According to Tokyo, Chicago and Detroit have been bombed till there is very little left. We get a big kick out of listening to the Jap broadcasts. They have one called "The Zero Hour." They play popular American tunes and interrupt every few minutes with remarks such as "How would you American soldiers like to be at home drinking an ice cold Coca-Cola?" — "How would you like to be at home with your girl with a big dish of ice cream?"

Love, Dave

July 22, 1943

Dear Aunt Eva and Uncle Bill:

This is the third day I have been anchored here. It is the longest rest I have had in weeks. My hand has finally gotten well, enough so that I can go swimming. It is a great relief to be able to get in the water and cool off. However, there is always the constant threat of sharks, so you never feel at ease. We also have crocodiles, but I have only seen two of them, so they don't worry me.

I think I got promoted to a lieutenant (J.G.) about a month ago, but we have never gotten the official word. We will probably be fighting the Japs over here after Washington signs the armistice. The news is so slow.

I wish I had more time to write you some of the human side of this war, and some of the funny incidents I have seen, but I guess I will have to wait until I get a leave or the war is over, and we gather around the fireplace with a few bottles of cold beer.

Love, Dave

July 25, 1943

Dear Mother and Dad:

I enjoy your letters very much, and appreciate your loyalty in writing so many. I try to appear to be hardened to the life and to being away from the States, to serve as an example to my men, but when I pull into port, I always know there will be mail waiting for me.

I don't know whether I told you that I got rid of my boatswain's mate and made Gorski my first mate again. I also got rid of Sneigouski. My hand has finally gotten well enough so I can go swimming, and I think that all I need is time to make it good as new.

A couple of lines that keep running through my mind:

"But that's all shoved behind me, long ago and fur away

And there ain't no girls to dance with on the Road to Mandalay."

"Lord, be thanked whate'er comes after, I have lived and toiled with men."

I wish I could remember the rest of that poem — You might send me an anthology of poetry.

Love, Dave

August 1, 1943

Dear Mother and Dad:

I have learned a great deal about war since I have been here. I believe it is the popular misconception that wars are won by men on the land with machine guns, and men in the air. A very small number of men ever do any actual fighting. Wars are won by supplies and the threat of force. We have large numbers of the fighting Marines who load and unload our barges. Most of them have never, and will never, use their rifles against the enemy. Almost all airplanes are good for is to shoot down the enemy's airplanes. As far as the bombing goes, it takes an awful lot of planes and bombs to make even a small dent on a small island. There is very little glamour or glory near the front. It is just a lot of hard work under difficult circumstances. The majority of men who are sent back as casualties are men whose health or nerves have broken down. The Japs crack up more planes every day on routine flights than Colin Kelly shot down. If everybody does their job every day, we will steam roller the Japs and win this war.

My hand is getting better all the time, but it will be a long time before it is as good as it was before.

One of my new men is a Jewish "Dead-end Kid" from Brooklyn. His name is Abe Melhamed, and he is twenty-one years old and weighs about ninety pounds. His rating says he is a pharmacist's mate, and he is supposed to take care of our casualties, but I wouldn't let him treat a slight case of trench-foot. I use him as a deck hand, and when he tells me that his job is "to keep as many men at as many guns, as many days as possible," I tell him to get out and swab the deck. His diction is almost difficult to understand. When he talks of Brooklyn, he says, "Geez, dat's a wunnerful location." The only reason that I keep him is that he is so dumb and impractical that he is good for the morale. He has little eyes that shine like buttons, and a very knowing smile. He spent the other afternoon telling how he would like to take out my appendix. That night Heyd caught a fish and Abe was afraid to take it off the hook. I think my appendix is safe from him for a while.

The other day we were loading several hundred Army troops that we were taking up to a fighting position. Suddenly a truck pulled up and a worn out looking coverall-clad band began to play. It was so incongruous that bystanders began to laugh. The band acted like they were being forced to play, and the soldiers acted like they were being forced to go. When they dragged out "Honeysuckle Road", I heard one of the soldiers say, "They ought to be playing 'Gloomy Sunday.'" It was the first band I had seen since I left the States. Somebody had the right idea, but it was like pouring a quart of water out in the middle of the desert. The only highlight was made by Abe, who was busily running in and out of the band like a little dog. When one of the soldiers in the band told him that they never went up to the line themselves — they just played for the soldiers that did, Abe's little button eyes shone, and he said, "Geez, dat's good duty." He immediately got his mouth organ and started practicing.

My other new man is Reeves, the electrician, who is 42 years old and has three children. He is big and strong, and has been a bum all of his life, so he can do practically anything. I have to watch him to see that he doesn't win from the other men all of their money, playing cards.

You have told me very little about your business, except that you have very little to do. How is the financial situation? Do you have any prospects for the future?

Love, Dave

August 6, 1943

Dear Mother and Dad:

I am back at a place where I can breathe freely again. My last trip was a very interesting one, as I went to an outpost where few boats have ever been. In fact, nobody had gone there since the day the place was taken. The men on the beach were really glad to see us. I have never been appreciated so much by anyone as I was by those fellows. They were almost entirely out of food, and I brought one hundred tons of that. It was the most picturesque place I have ever been. You really had to know where you were going to find it.

I was not only the captain of a ship when I got there, I was the captain of *the* ship. We had just made a big haul before we went there, from a big ship that didn't know the value of fresh food. We had fresh meat, eggs, butter, etc. The food which we brought the base was of course all dehydrated, but I allowed a few special guests to eat aboard my ship and partake of the fresh food. I enjoyed the party very much.

Life has been easy this last month; the fresh food we got has helped a lot. I look forward to a busy month the last half of August and September. We are very interested in the war out here; when we take another base there is great rejoicing.

Love, Dave

September 6, 1943

Dear Mother and Dad:

Two days ago, I received quite a bit of mail. I am very happy to hear of Dad's rapid recovery. You say it is hot in K.C. — well, it is hotter here than any place I have ever been, but it cools off at night. I have not had the malaria, but I have had the dysentery, which is otherwise known as the bloody flux. Most of the diseases in the South Pacific were first noticed on the island of Tulagi, and they received their names there.

I caught up with the fighting men about ten days ago, and have been operating there steady since then. It has been the hardest ten days I ever had on a boat. I have hit more reefs than I hoped I would in the rest of my life. Right now, I am limping back to the temporary base we have set up, on one and one half engines, instead of my usual three. The waters here are so unreliable and treacherous, that I can't afford to leave the bridge for hours at a time. LCT are the only boats which could possibly operate here. I don't know who is getting the credit for winning the war, but the LCTs and the bulldozers are the ones that are doing it. In half of the invasions they put off a bulldozer with a Seabee on it to make a path through the jungle for the commandoes to invade on.

I have enjoyed the poetry Dad has sent very much, and I appreciate your trouble in copying it. I think all of my trouble has been caused by my raising a mustache, and although my men say I look like Douglas Fairbanks, Jr. with it, I will shave it off tomorrow.

Love, Dave

September 14, 1943

Dear Ann:

I received your letter of the 27th yesterday. I was going to write you a nice long letter, but the cook just came in and informed me that the port hold is full of water and we are sinking by the bow. (How do you like my nautical language?) That is the compartment where we stow our food, so I guess I better do something quick. He says the provisions are floating in a foot of water now, and the water is rising rapidly. If I hadn't just finished my breakfast, I could take more interest in the food problem.

There is nothing hard about this war. It is only the people you have to fight it with that make it tough. Now if I had a crew made up of you and Thorne and Eddie Gitz and Jay and Bill and Kippie and Aunt Eva and Harold and Bettie, and Grandma Newty, we could fight the Japs in the daytime and drink beer and sing songs at night. It would be a regular picnic, and I wouldn't have to listen to people arguing all day about whether Harry James was good enough for Betty Grable. Personally, I think anybody is good enough for Betty Grable, and I don't care to discuss it.

They just brought out twenty men they are loaning me for the day to help get my boat in shape to go back to the front. We are now painting the boat's bottom and welding the holes I knocked into it. I am also getting new propellers and so on. They are in a terrific hurry to get me back to the front, so I can run onto another reef.

Ann, I have to go. The cook says the damned boat really is sinking. I wish you a lot of luck this year at school. If you send me your address, I will write you a nice, long letter.

Love, Dave

September 16, 1943

Dear Mother and Dad:

One of my good friends over here, who is also an LCT skipper, had a wonderful experience last week. We are all quite envious. He was sent on a tour with his boat to some of the little known islands that the war hasn't touched. He was to go to the native villages with his interpreter and ask the natives to gather coconut thatch. It was to be used to build warehouses. He was to go from one village to another until he had a boatload of it. He got back yesterday, after being gone ten days, and of the stories I've heard so far, his are the wildest. Of the natives he met, many had never seen a white man, and almost none had seen an American. Everywhere he went, he was lavishly entertained. He brought back enough souvenirs to outfit a museum. At one of the villages he was invited to stay for supper and dancing. No one in the village could speak English; his interpreter had to interpret everything. After supper, the chief had the tribe sing for him. They sang several native songs. Then, without any change of expression or change of tune, they sang about six verses of "She'll be coming round the mountain when she comes." The natives had no idea what the words meant. When the natives finished singing, the officer had his men (he had brought six with him) sing a few songs for the natives. They sang three or four, ending up with the "Marine Hymn." They kind of petered out on the hymn, because most of the boys didn't know the words. Before they had finished, there were only one or two men singing. When they finished, there was quiet for a minute. Then the whole native village burst into song — the "Marine Hymn." They knew the words and they knew the tune. They sang it very well.

A native here buys his wife from his future father-in-law. A native approached Mr. Jones, our commanding officer, one day, and said he was in serious trouble. It seems he had bought his wife on the installment plan, and had failed to make the payments. His father-in-law had taken the man's wife away from him. Mr. Jones helped Ben make the payments, and Ben has been Mr. Jones' devoted servant ever since. Mr. Jones asked Ben to bring his wife around, so he could see her. The native village is located about five miles back in the hills. The next day, Ben brought his wife. The women here do not wear any clothes above the waist, but Ben is a pretty smart native, and he had his wife dressed for the occasion. She had on two Navy bath towels. Right across her breast and right across her behind, in big letters it said, "U.S. NAVY."

Love, Dave

October 4, 1943

Dear Mother and Dad,

This letter writing has gotten to be somewhat of a problem for me. Although I am not reporting the action of the war, as I am not allowed to say what I see, all I have left to write about are the little incidents that make up our everyday life out here. I feel sure you are interested, and I enjoy writing about them.

Last night, I had a long talk with a young would-be-intellectual ensign, who confided to me that he was going to write a book telling what it is really like out here, when he gets back to the States. He maintained that if the people back in the States knew about the terrible blunders that had been made out here by some of our military leaders, they would be astonished. He went on to enumerate many things, examples of lack of foresight and organization, sacrifices of men and materials, conditions under which men lived that were bad for health and morale. When he got through, he had just about convinced himself that all of the generals and admirals ought to be court-martialed.

I had a very strong negative reaction to this man. I have seen enough to know that the generals and admirals are working their heads off along with everyone else, and I would say of the whole situation, "We are doing as well as could be expected." There have been many blunders made, and no one has seen them any more than I have. I made one trip to the extreme front lines that was rather dangerous, and my total load consisted of tons of fly paper. I have made several trips to far flung isolated outposts with food — only to discover that half of the food in my load was rotten. There are many more that I could tell of, but no one group is responsible.

If anyone is to be blamed for anything, it should be the relationship of a democracy to war. I am glad to live in a democracy. Anyone who is, has to be willing to make those sacrifices which are caused by the weaknesses of one. Whenever a democracy organizes a huge fighting machine overnight, there are bound to be misunderstandings and incompetent people scattered throughout. As I have said before, we will steamroller our enemies, and win this war. I believe we would be better organized, and win it sooner, if we lived in a dictatorship, but who wants to live in a dictatorship? I don't.

Love, Dave

October 13, 1943

Dear Mother and Dad:

We have been relieved, and are going back down the line. It is time we are going back to our base, as we are out of food and fuel. Goforth has been running a temperature for a couple of days, and is in bed. York got burnt in the engine room today, when a line broke and he got sprayed with hot steam. We are out of gasoline to run our rubber boat on hunting trips. We are out of lube oil. Our fishing tackle is all gone.

I think the story of the week is that we came back from the most advanced outpost the Americans have with our icebox crammed full of fresh meat, while the boys who sit back in civilized area where the ships come in, are all eating Spam and Vienna sausage. They couldn't understand it. We ate so much Spam and Vienna sausage when we first came out here that we learned to hate it. When the ships started bringing fresh meat, it was very much appreciated. Some of these islands had large plantations on them before the war; some had a few cattle. However, we found an island up the line where there were still a few cattle running around. Well, to make a long story short, Heyd and Cookie (a very capable ex-farmer) came back from a hunting trip one day with the body of a cow in the rubber boat. They had shot him and cut his head off. I was kind of leery of it, not only because it seemed like rustling, but also because there was no sign on it, "Government Inspected." However, we have eaten about half of that cow now and I am feeling fine.

I have thought of my family in many different ways since I have been out here, ways that I never thought on before. Raising a large family is in many ways similar to running a ship. It would be impossible for me to run the ship if there was another officer who had equal authority with me. We would be continually giving contradictory orders. In our family, and as far as I can remember, there were no contradictory orders. One of the requirements of a good officer is the ability to say "no" to one of his favorite men. This is also necessary in a parent. It must be extremely hard sometimes, when they love their children a great deal. The hardest job on this boat is keeping it clean and doing the dishes. I wonder sometimes how Mother used to keep that big house clean. Even when she had a maid, it was no snap. I have one boy on mess duty a week at a time. He does the dishes and swabs out the living quarters every day, but he can't keep the place clean unless the other boys help him.

Well, it is time to go to bed now. Another day, another dollar, and another day closer to when I will come home.

Love, Dave

November 2, 1943

Dear Mother and Dad —

I guess you realize that on the 23rd of last month, I had been out of the United States for six full months. On the fourth of this month, I will have been a skipper for one year. Back home, Georgie is seventeen years old and winter is coming on. The girls are wearing sweaters and skirts; the leaves are on the ground and Thanksgiving will soon be here. But out here, time passes by unnoticed because there are no seasons. We always wear the same clothes (literally speaking), eat the same food and look at the same kind of trees. The coconut trees have just one season and that lasts for twelve months.

Last week we made a trip back from one of the advanced bases with a Navy doctor as a passenger. There were no other passengers and the ship was empty. There was a larger ship going back with us and I advised him to ride on it which had much nicer quarters. But he refused as he said he had ridden up on that ship and it had made him sea sick. I felt sorry for him in his ignorance, but everyone must learn. On the way down, we ran into one of the roughest storms we have been in. It started about 12:30 at night. Shortly after I had closed my eyes, my whole library, which is in several bookshelves at the head of my bunk, came down on me. With them came about a dozen phonograph records which we had stored up there. It was pitch dark in the quarters and the books and records made quite an impression on me. Among the things that went were almost all our dishes, and our radio. This was quite a shock to me as it is a very expensive instrument. But everything that is issued to an LCT is expendable and I do not have to account for everything. If it breaks we throw is over the side and they give us another if they have it. The thing that got the Doctor was the anchor banging against the stern. He thought it was going through the bulkhead.

The highlight of the night came when the rudder stuck on hard right rudder. One of the chains running from the wheel to the rudder had come off the sprocket and jammed. We had it fixed inside half an hour but in the meantime we made a couple of rough circles. That doctor carried a story of the LCT back to his hospital which did us a lot of good. They treat every LCT man that enters that hospital with the greatest of respect.

I saw a movie tonight which is a rare thing for me. I am disgusted with the movies they send out here. Tonight, it was "Five Graves to Cairo," a lousy war propaganda show. The last three shows I have seen have been either war propaganda thrillers in which the Germans or the Japs kill either the hero or the heroine. I don't go to the show to see people get killed and I think it is a crime to send that trash out here.

My old electrician who was forty-two years old and had three children was sent back to the States as his health gave out. My new electrician is a twenty year old boy named Butch from Topeka, Kansas. The other day he fell off the top of the wheel house and hit on the main deck. I thought he was dead. We got him into a plane and they flew him to the nearest hospital. The next day they flew him back with the notation that there was nothing wrong with him. Now, all the boys want to fall off so they can get a plane ride.

I received the two books of Kipling's poems and am enjoying them very much. I realize it was a great concession as they contain many of the best. I also received Georgia's cartoon book and Mother's pajamas. I think they are the coolest pajamas I have ever seen and I enjoy them very much.

———————

Six hours late, with our motors held together with everything the kitchen could provide, we steamed into our destination. All the motors were running and all the bells were buzzing. I have had a few temporary repairs and am ready to start back now. As soon as we get there I am going to ask for two new engines. I think that these two have done their share for the war effort.

I try to keep my room neat, but I am handicapped because I wasn't trained right in my youth. So, occasionally a stray article gets on the deck. Red, who is a very neat person, stopped in front of my room yesterday and with a very surprised look on his face said "What happened, Skipper? Did you have a fight in there?" He walked on before I could say anything, but I cleaned my room up.

Time to shove off — Dave

November 8, 1943

Dear Mother and Dad —

We are back at our base at last. I don't care to go through such an experience again. At one time on the way back, we had only the port engine started. Even our generator went out on the way back which took away our lights, stove, icebox, fans, etc. I am at the base now and have issued an ultimatum that I won't move without two new engines. I think I will get them tomorrow.

We have been able to get our hands on quite a few cases of beer lately. We stole a reefer box from the PT boys and it is a great big ice box. We keep it stocked full of beer now and the cook keeps the key. Whenever I give the word, we have a grog ration. Whenever we survive a bad storm, I order double rations.

We never go near Guadalcanal and it's a good thing as we don't have any uniforms that are nice enough.

It is time for me to go to bed now. I have a busy day tomorrow getting my ship in shape so I can go out and knock myself out again.

Love, Dave

P.S. As for your reference to Thomas Wolfe, I tried to read *Of Time and The River* about a month ago and I quit at the end of the first hundred pages. I don't know whether the book was inferior to his others, or whether my taste has changed or whether I am so flighty I can't concentrate on anything.

November 23, 1943

Dear Mother and Dad —

I have been working hard lately but we have had pretty good luck with our motors and the weather. Gorski went to the hospital with infected heat blisters and that makes my job a little harder.

On this last trip I made, I carried thirty-two New Zealand soldiers on top of the load for three days. They wanted to go to an out-of-the-way island and since we were going past it, we took them along. They are a very interesting people. I have always admired Ronald Coleman in the movies so much. Well, I had Ronald Colemans sitting all over my load. Neat as a pin, conservative and quiet, and very polite.

The first lieutenant took care of his men as if they were on a Sunday school picnic. He made each man change his clothes after it rained. He helped them make their beds and he counted them three times a day. He did everything for them but blow their noses and I came to the conclusion that Ronald Coleman was a wonderful man for some woman to take care of and love, but he would certainly be out of place in the rough, loud, vulgar, capable American army. The lieutenant took care of the soldiers and I wondered who was going to take care of the lieutenant. He was just like an old woman who worried about everything and fussed all the time but never actually did anything.

During the trip, we had a crate of oranges, which are priceless out here, sitting right out on the deck, but not a one was stolen. Any American outfit we have carried would have stolen them all. When we unloaded the New Zealanders and their gear, their friends on the beach came aboard and helped them unload. After they had gone, we discovered that our oranges and many other things were gone. Their friends were not as honest as they were. We learned a little lesson there. There are honest and dishonest people in every outfit regardless of nationality.

Love, Dave

Dec 6, 1943

Dear Mother and Dad;

My experiences this last month have been numerous and varied. But since the censorship regulations forbid descriptions of experiences in fighting the Japs, I will have to be content with telling you of my experiences in fighting the Americans.

About a week ago (maybe it was two weeks), I was underway on an all night trip. I was the lead boat in a group of three LCT's. It was a very dark night and I had gone to bed at two a.m. dead tired. I was awakened at quarter-to-four by a terrific crash that threw me out of my bunk. I was sleeping skinny up and I ran up on the bridge without putting my clothes on. My men were all over the bridge shouting at each other. I could see the shadow of another ship that was obvious. When I inquired, "What did we hit?" the first answer I got was, "We hit a Jap submarine that was surfaced."

Nobody knew what kind of ship it was or how it had happened. Abe, the little Jewish pharmacist mate, was shouting "general quarters, man the guns." I was peering into the darkness saying, "Wait till I see what it is." Abe said, "Shoot the son of a bitch and then see what it is."

I finally recognized the type of ship it was and knew it was one of ours. I thought it was one of our fast new ships that are made out of wood and my first thought was that it was probably sinking. No one knew how the accident had occurred and I thought we had probably come up from behind him and rammed him. Finally, he started signaling to me by blinker, and his first message was, "Where did I hit you?"

I was so happy I started clapping my hands. He thought he had hit me. I didn't answer his message.

I ignored it, and sent him the message, "Where are you hurt?"

He sent back, "In the bow."

I began to relax and went down after my pants and shoes. When I arrived at Guadalcanal the next morning, I bummed a jeep ride to the amphibious headquarters and reported the accident. When I started telling the story to the admiral's flag secretary, he stopped me and said I might as well tell it to the admiral. The admiral continued to eat his breakfast of corn flakes while I reported the incident. When I finished, he looked up and said, "Did anybody get hurt?"

"I don't know. No one on my ship did."

"Well, I don't think it was your fault. In the first place, he had radar and you didn't. And, in the second place, if you hadn't hit him one of the other LCTs would have.

"We are loading up to land on a new island, and we have a tough assignment for you. You forget about the accident. You are doing a great job. Go back to your ship and continue doing it." I decided they needed me and my boat too much to worry about the wrecks I have.

It is a funny thing, but when I ran up on deck that night, stark naked, with the noise of the collision and the shouting of the crew in my ears and the feeling that we were entirely to blame, the first thing I thought of was Billy Shofstall's father's car. My first instinct was, "This is a hell of a mess. I better call my dad to straighten it out."

I have a disease called the Tulagi Rot. It has been a long time since I saw the place where the name of this disease originated, but the disease seems to be all over the South Seas. It started on my most vulnerable spot, my nose, and it is still spreading. Abe has been treating it unsuccessfully for three days and yesterday I found a Marine doctor. He was pretty busy but he got out a bottle of Gentian Violet and painted my face a deep purple. I look like something out of a circus. He made the remark, "That ought to hold it. It has been so long since I practiced medicine that I can't remember the name of these diseases." That was a very reassuring thing to tell me. I wondered if he had been digging ditches from the last ten years and just pressed into the medical service for the emergency. I am now on the hunt for another doctor who remembers the names of the diseases. Any Latin phrases he can give me will help my peace of mind.

My boat is running well now, and we have covered many miles of water in the last month.

Don't worry about me. One of these days before you know it, I will sail the battle scarred old "324" right down Kansas City's Wornall Road.

Love, Dave

December 8, 1943

Dear Mother and Dad —

I have just finished reading *The Dollar Gold Piece* and tonight my mind is full of Quality Hill and the old Coates House. I didn't care much for the plot but I enjoyed the K.C. setting very much.

I have had a very exciting day myself. Yesterday, I had to beach in the middle of quite a storm. In order to keep from broaching on the beach, I let my anchor out as I went it. In backing off the beach, I committed the sailor's impardonable sin of catching my own anchor cable in my screw. It stopped the screw instantly and I narrowly avoided broaching on the beach. This morning, I tried to dive down and tie a line on to the anchor, but I found the anchor was hanging too far down. I couldn't stand the pressure, so I borrowed a diving helmet from a PT boat outfit. It was one that sat on your shoulders and was equipped with an air pump and hose. I was able to get down to the anchor with this helmet on, and through a system of trials and errors, freed the line. Best of all, I won today what Dad would call a moral victory. We got that cable free without any outside assistance in a locality where outside assistance would be very difficult to get. I have seen those diving helmets used in the movies, but I have never seen them used in the shark- infested waters of the combat area.

A couple days after Christmas I received so many packages that I will never get the thank you letters written. We shoved off that night and in the confusion I am not at all sure who sent me what. I got a box from Sally Winkworth, Mrs. Archer, Nancy Goodman, Auntie Joe, George and Harriett, Mrs. Gray and there might be some more that I don't remember. They contained mostly candy, soap, cigarettes and a few unusable articles of clothing. One box contained six black neckties. I haven't worn one since I left the States. Mrs. Archer sent me the last pair of rubber suspenders in K.C. I appreciate them no end, but they look kind of funny when you don't wear a shirt.

I am trying to get around to sending some of my extra clothes home in a box. So if a box of my old clothes arrives, don't think that is all that remains of the body.

Dad mentioned an identification bracelet in one of his letters. I guess it would be a good thing to have as I have lost my dog tags and unless my pants had a laundry tag in them, I wouldn't be recognized floating around dead. I never thought it made much difference whether you were recognized or not as long as you were dead. If you have it made, put on it "blood type O." I guess I must be pretty lifeless with blood type zero.

Love, Dave

P.S. We had fish for dinner and I am enclosing part of his teeth. He was a barracuda I think.

The Solomon Islands

In December of 1943, I had an experience that I did not write home about as I didn't think the censor would pass it.

My LCT was unloading ships at Bougainville. The island of Bougainville was on the northern end of the Solomon Islands. We had carried the Marines ashore here and they had driven the Japs back and established a beachhead. The island was over a hundred miles long and about thirty miles wide. The Japs still held the major portion of the island but the Marines had cut out a perimeter that was big enough to have a base camp and a landing strip.

We were bringing in the ammunition, food and other supplies from the ships standing off the coast. When I came into the beach there was a Marine colonel waiting to talk to me. We talked on the bridge while they were unloading the ship. He said he needed an LCT skipper to volunteer for a special trip and Captain Kessing on the beach had recommended "Wavey Davey" for the job. He had said, "Hawley is so miserable with the jungle rot on his face, he hasn't got much to lose." I had my face painted purple with Gentian Violet at this time.

The colonel said a small Marine detachment had penetrated the Jap lines and gone inland to determine the strength and which Jap units were on Bougainville. Now they were ready to come back and they thought it would be safer for them to get picked up on the beach than to come back though the front lines. They were close to the beach about fifteen miles north of our beach. If we could come up the coast about a mile out, they would set off a purple smoke bomb when we got opposite them. The colonel said he would go with us.

As soon as they got the LCT unloaded, we started up the coast. We looked at our chart to help us guess where the Marines were and three men including the colonel watched the shore with binoculars for the smoke bomb.

"There it is." The colonel had spotted the smoke bomb.

I headed into the beach at a right angle. I realized there was a reef about one hundred and fifty yards off the beach and I thought I could go on over it. We would hit the reef with our bottom but the momentum of the LCT would carry it over the reef and into the deep water on the other side. We continued across this water to the beach. There was a fifty foot sand beach with solid jungle on the other side. I had told my crew not to man the guns, but to stay out of sight. We had learned that when someone shoots at you out of the jungle, you don't know where to shoot back.

We dropped the ramp and here came the Marines. They had about a hundred and fifty feet of beach to cover and somebody was shooting at them. One of them fell. I couldn't tell whether he tripped or had been shot. He never had time to find out. Two big Marines grabbed him under either arm and dragged him almost as fast as they could run. Everybody was aboard and the ramp was on its way up. "All engines full astern. Take up on the anchor winch. Don't back over the cable."

We came off the beach easily. We bounced over the reef and headed for our anchor. As soon as we got the anchor up, we headed down the coast far enough out so they wouldn't shoot at us with rifles. When we started down the coast, the Marines were all below getting something to eat. Pretty soon the second lieutenant in charge of the Marines came up on the bridge and stood beside me. I saw he was one of the two men who had carried the man that fell. He said to me, "I understand from the colonel, that you volunteered for this job. I just want to say thank you."

"Don't thank me. Thank the colonel. He pressured me into coming after you. He told me how valuable the info was you had collected."

"When he told you how valuable the info was, did he also tell you he was my father?"

"I don't remember him telling me that."

"It's a fact. He isn't even in our outfit. We were supposed to reenter the American perimeter the same way we went out. Picking us up on the beach was his idea. I'll admit it was a lot easier and a lot safer, thanks to you."

January 19, 1944

Dear Mother and Dad —

The pressure has been put upon us. I have done harder work with my boat and worked longer hours this last two weeks than ever before. It certainly shows on my boat too. Among other things, I have five holes in the bulkhead beside my bunk and when we get our daily rain, my bunk gets its daily soaking.

I wrote and told you how I got an anchor cable fouled in my screw a week or so ago. Two days after that, I got a cargo net fouled in my screw. We caught it at four-thirty one afternoon and at six a.m. the next morning I was operating again.

The day after I got the net unfouled, I had a head-on collision with a boat similar to mine only smaller, faster and made of wood. His boat sunk within five minutes of the collision. They decided I was blameless and court-martialed the other guy. By the way, I heard the other day that the skipper of that ship I collided with a couple months ago got court-martialed. I heard one officer say the other day, "The safest place to be when Hawley is around is on his boat."

The long hours and the rough seas have taken a heavy toll on the men's energy and nerves. They fight among themselves over the work and they make me mad and then I fly off the handle. I can never remember losing my temper before I joined the Navy. Now, I have one just like Dad's. I have the most trouble with my engineers, York and Anderson. York is the leader of the two and a crack engineer but I can hardly stand to be around him anymore. We have lived in the same room for fifteen months. We live so close together that when we have to work unreasonably long hard hours and our bodies and nerves are worn out, it is so easy to step on somebody else's toes. Also, everybody's faults are so apparent when they live like this. Up here it rains every day and our living quarters are always damp if not actually wet. The wind blows continually so the barge is pitching and tossing all day and night.

There are a lot of soldiers out here that have lived like pigs too long. Some of these outfits have been out of the States for three years. These are National Guard outfits and they were pretty sorry to start with. They unload us sometimes and you can tell by their eyes and facial movements that a lot of them are nervous wrecks. People don't call them nervous wrecks; they call them crazy. My cook made a startling announcement today when he said, "Maybe we are crazy, too. We haven't seen anybody to talk to for so long that we might be and not know it."

I have got a lot of good books and good poetry books. They are a blessing to me. Sometimes I have a little time off but I am too tired and nervous to sleep. However, I pick up a good book and forget my troubles. I have three or four anthologies of poetry beside my numerous volumes of Kipling. I don't know how I am going to get these books back home unless I build a box and send them in advance. However, if they were to offer to let me go home just as I am in my underwear I would leave everything including my grass skirts and medal. My clothes are no good. My uniforms are ruined by the damp weather.

Well, one of these days I will settle down in the davenport at home to tell you of my adventures in the South Sea. I won't be able to remember anything except I was very busy.

All my love, Dave

January 25, 1944

Dear Mother and Dad —

One of our troubles has been eliminated. Some general had a washing machine sent to him from the States. He was unfortunate enough to be sent to the front before it arrived and we transshipped it. I begged those boys to leave that washing machine alone but I might as well have tried to take food away from a starving man. It has never stopped running for a week. They have washed everything in sight. Many of these boys come from families that never had a washing machine and to them it is almost black magic. At least, my clothes are all clean now and I guess they will stay clean if the machine holds up. The boys said the general probably never did anything to get his clothes dirty anyway.

I will be going back to the base soon and I will be glad to see the end of this duty as it has been rough. I will probably be a couple weeks in getting repaired.

I have received no mail since Dec. 27 as they don't send mail up here. It will be waiting for me when I get back to the base.

Love, Dave

March 4, 1944

Dear Mother and Dad —

I have a sty on my eye and ought to go to bed, but if I don't write you pretty soon you will begin to think I am on my way home and this is far from true. I am back up at the front again and fighting the weather, bugs, skin disease etc. I lost a screw yesterday and backed up on the beach to put a new one on. I got the new screw on and now I can't get off the beach. I hope to get off at high tide tomorrow morning.

Tonight I went to some boxing matches between the Army and the Navy. They almost had to call it off because the supporters of both teams were a little too demonstrative. One of the referees got beat up something awful. The Navy couldn't stand to see a sailor get whipped by a "dog face." Those fights tonight were within hearing distance of the Japanese guns, but they might as well have been ten thousand miles away.

The highlight of last week occurred when I attended church Sunday morning in a front line church. There were about two hundred men there, sailors, Army, and Marines. It was a very good sermon by a young Episcopalian minister, but most of the men in that congregation were Baptists. When I thought back, I was positive that every time I have attended church out here, the majority of the congregation has been Baptists. It must be kind of hard on these ministers from Episcopalian

High Church to come out here and preach to the back woods Baptists like me.

At present I expect to go home in May, but that is indefinite. Mr. Bud Jones finally went back to the States and instead of giving us the Princeton man I had expected, we got Mr. Decateur Jones who was my CO while I was in San Francisco. He just took over this week so I don't know what his policy will be, but I have heard that he is scared to death that Mr. Bud Jones is going to take all the experienced men out of here and leave him with a bunch of green officers. Therefore, he is not a supporter of the relief program. Time will tell.

My crew has been getting along pretty well. Gorski has developed into a pretty good second in command and has taken a lot of the responsibility off of my shoulders. I find that he can get along with some of the people I have trouble with.

Mother said in one of her letters that Jimmy Winkworth was engaged. Is this a fact. I wonder if Thorne Gray has any boy friends. I might as well add her to my list. I am getting tired of the ones I have.

We are about over the rainy season and the weather is calming down. I am enjoying good health and so far the work has not been hard this trip. I am getting awfully tired of the dehydrated food and this perpetual summer, but I could continue to survive under these conditions for a long time if I had to. Boy, what I wouldn't give for some cool Autumn days in Missouri. I also could go for a chocolate milkshake and a bacon and tomato sandwich in a big way. This continued heat is hard on my appetite.

I finally packed those clothes I am going to sent home and will mail them at first opportunity. When I painted Kansas City, Missouri U.S.A. on that suitcase, I got bang out of it.

Love, Dave

Back to the States

We were still unloading ships at Bougainville in April of '44 when my orders come to return to the United States. My replacement brought the orders. He said he had flown in on a DC-3 and if I hurried I could catch it on its return trip to the Russel Islands. He also said they were talking about closing the airstrip when he left there. I immediately started packing. What should I take home? I pulled my box from under my bunk and started throwing things in it.

"Where are you going?" I looked up and saw Heyd and Gorski watching me.

I said, "I have been relieved and am being sent back to San Francisco for reassignment. Lt. Taylor here is replacing me."

Red Gothardt was standing behind Gorski and Heyd said, "What happens to us?"

I said, "You will continue to do your job until you are relieved, which I hope will be soon." All of a sudden I felt like, "How can I leave these guys? Can they make it without me?"

I felt like I raised them and taught them everything they knew. They looked up to me. They depended on me. I was leaving them a long way from home. On the bumpy plane ride down to the Russels, I decided I was overestimating their dependence on me. All of a sudden, I was free of the responsibility. I was a free agent.

When I walked into Decateur Jones' office and asked how soon I could leave for the United States, he said, "What's your hurry?"

"I have in my hand orders that say Lt. Hawley will proceed to San Francisco where he will receive orders that send him on leave." Decateur Jones who was our new flotilla commander was an old friend of mine.

He said, "Sit down, Dave; lets talk about this. If you are like everybody that had gone before you, you are going to be disappointed and let down. Unless you have a wife or sweetheart waiting for you, which I am pretty sure don't, you are going to find that all your friends are gone except your folks. After the life you have been living, about the second day, you are going to find it a little slow."

"So?"

"Why don't you stay here a few days and wind down before you leave? It won't count on your leave. The best friends you have in this world are on this island. Nobody enjoys playing poker and drinking beer more than you do. You can bunk up there at the BOQ and sleep in the daytime until you are caught up on your sleep. It's just a suggestion. You can leave today if you want to."

"That might not be a bad idea. I'll stay tonight anyway and try it out."

We didn't have any gambling on the LCT but every time we got back to our base, I would spend the evening playing poker with the other skippers and members of the staff whose LCTs were in the harbor. I had made a rule for myself that any night that I lost a hundred dollars, I quit for that night. I never broke that rule. I stayed five nights and I lost five hundred dollars. Then, I went into Mr. Jones again and told him I had enjoyed the hospitality very much but I couldn't afford it. I was ready to go home.

Bob Willits went with Harvey Shuler, a fellow LCT skipper, and me to Guadalcanal to catch a freighter home. We stood on the beach waiting for a small boat to take us out to our cargo ship and Willits proposed we go odd man, shooting craps, one time for a hundred dollars. We did it and Willits won. Harvey said, "Let's go one more time." We did and Harvey won. Willits said he didn't feel right about "Wavey" losing two hundred dollars and them both winning. "Let's go one more time and give him a chance to be even." We went one more time and he won. We shook hands and left. Three hundred dollars is a lot of money to lose in five minutes when you only make one hundred twenty-five dollars a month.

When Shuler and I boarded the cargo ship for our trip home we found we had several fellow passengers. One of them was a chief signalman from the *President Adams*, Edward H. Rogers, Jr. I had done business with him and liked him. There was another LCT skipper named Marcel Graunard. He was a Frenchman from a sugar plantation just north of New Orleans. I liked him, too. There were six more Navy officers all with a lot of time overseas, and one Army officer. It took this Merchant Marine cargo ship a little over two weeks to cross the same ocean that it had required thirty-one days for us to cross a year earlier. The seas were calm and the skies were sunny. No one was in a hurry, but we tried several games to while away the time. The one we played the most was hopscotch. Shuler drew the game with a piece of chalk on the metal deck and announced he would play anybody for a buck a game. We all had lots of money which we didn't value very highly. Pretty soon, we were playing hopscotch for five dollars a game.

The meals were good and in the evening, the Merchant officers played poker. They welcomed Shuler and me into their game and I never had better luck. I enjoyed the trip.

Two of the passengers were Mustangs. A Mustang is a Naval officer who was an enlisted man for some time before he became a commissioned officer. They were named Taylor and Howell. Both of them were married and lived in the San Francisco Bay area. Another officer, Woolsi, was married and his wife was going to be in San Francisco waiting, although she didn't know what day we would get there. He said he and his wife were Mormons and she wasn't willing to expose him to the temptations in San Francisco without her. I knew Frances Hubbard would be waiting for me. It wouldn't surprise me if she was waiting on the pier.

By the time we were close enough to see the Golden Gate Bridge, we had gotten pretty good at hopscotch and were playing it for more money than we would ever play for again. Shuler and I had won most of the Merchant officers' money at poker, and my health had definitely benefitted from the two weeks cruise.

Six of us, Shuler, Rogers, Graunard, and an officer named Leslie and me and another hopscotch player rented a suite that had three bedrooms and a living room. The Mormon found his wife and got a room adjoining ours. She said, "You would think that he had seen enough of you guys."

After we had gorged ourselves, we reported in to the Navy. The pretty Wave officer that interviewed me said that they had left me in too long. She said in my type of duty, running a landing ship, you were supposed to be relieved at the end of six months. Consequently, *I would not have to go overseas.* I could pick the location of my duty for the rest of the war. I said I would like to be stationed at the Navy Air Base at Olathe, Kansas. She said for me to keep in touch as my orders would be received in about five days.

I had called Frances Hubbard when we got our hotel rooms and now she joined us. As usual she was full of good ideas that would keep us from spending our time in bars. I was now surrounded by men that I liked and who liked me.

My hopscotch playing friends never got tired of hearing my sea stories. I had a pretty girl who had written me the best letters I had ever received, and she was available morning, noon, and night. She had a good job and her boss was very understanding. I had honorably completed my duty in the Pacific War Zone and returned unscathed to San Francisco, one of the greatest fun cities in the U.S.

It was five days before my orders came, and they were five wonderful days. I spent money like a drunken sailor because that is what I was. Every day Frances would bring us a choice of things to do. We really saw the town and I loved it. The only thing that bothered me a little was that I felt Frances was pushing for some sort of commitment. She was wanting to get me alone so we could do some serious talking. I felt that Frances didn't really know me. This was a very artificial life that I knew was very temporary. Anybody looks good that is a returning war hero with lots of recognition from his peers, plenty of money to spend and not a care in the world. I kept telling her, "I expect to live a very dull life in Kansas City when this war is over." She was obviously a smart, aggressive person who was going to make something of her life. I didn't want to be married to somebody who was expecting great things of me and made me feel guilty. My orders came and I kissed her goodbye and got on the plane.

My mother and father knew that I was back in the United States but they didn't know when I would be coming home and I didn't tell them. I wanted to see their surprised looks. I walked up to the front door without a word of warning. Our door was never locked so I opened it and walked in. My mother was seated at her desk in the living room paying bills. When I said, "Hello, Mother," she looked up and said, "Oh, good. I have been needing somebody to go to the grocery store. I will make you a list."

Every time I went out of the house, my father wanted to go with me. When I announced one morning that I was going swimming, he yelled at my mother, "Lucille, where is my swimming suit?"

The orders that had sent me home, had said that I was to have a thirty-day leave and then I was to report to the commanding officer of the Olathe Air Base. After I had been home on leave for ten days, I received a telegram from the Bureau of Personnel in Washington, D.C. It said I was to report immediately to the Amphibious Training Base in Little Creek, Virginia. I was to undergo a training course that would prepare me to take command of the LSM 59, Landing Ship-Medium, which was under construction. I was not thrilled to learned that I was going back to the Pacific, but I had wondered how I was going to fit in with the dry land sailors at the air base. I had learned that Keith Trotter from William Jewell was stationed in Olathe and he had taken me out to a local watering spot where a large number of the ship's company from the airbase hung out. They wore the same uniform I did but they didn't speak the same language or feel the same about the war. I had felt that night like a fish out of water. So, it was with mixed feelings that I said goodbye to my folks and got on the train.

June 4, 1944

Dear Mother and Dad,

I have been extremely busy getting oriented to my new life. I am to be the commanding officer of one of the new

LSM ships. I am to spend ten weeks here training, six weeks ashore, and two weeks afloat. I go to school seven days a week. Among my other classes, I have to master navigation during this time. I will have to diligently apply myself, as the other members of the class took navigation in midshipman's school. At the conclusion of the ten-week training program, I take my crew to the shipyard, where my ship is being built. You can see I am going to be a busy man.

Love, Dave

When I left the Amphibious Training Base at Little Creek twenty months before, it was in the process of being built. There was deep mud everywhere and no one was sure what they were supposed to be doing. Now, everything was highly organized. The hours in the classrooms were very long and the novelty soon wore off for me. Every third night, our school stopped at six o'clock and I spent those evenings with my old friend Elizabeth "Lyba" McPherin. She was the first real Southern lady I had known well and I liked her a lot. Her mother and dad treated me like a long-lost son.

There were four officers assigned to my ship's company besides myself: an engineering officer, the gunnery and supply officer and a third officer. The fourth officer was the executive officer who was supposed to be my right hand man. I don't remember his name because he was trying to get re-assigned to some other duty from the day that I met him. When I found this out, I wrote a long letter to the Bureau of Personnel in Washington, D.C. I told them what my history was and said I did not want this job. However, if I had to have the job, the least they could do for me was to assign me an executive officer that could help me and with whom

I could get along. I suggested Edward H. Rogers, Jr. Rogers showed up at the Amphibious Base at Little Creek dragging his sea bag behind him. He was furious. He had always made fun of the LCTs, LCIs, and LSTs, and claimed they were not part of the real Navy. At first, he was sullen and cynical. Later on, he was just cynical. Writing that letter and getting Rogers assigned as my executive officer was the smartest thing I did during my Naval career.

I was not used to sitting all day in school and some of my instructors were teaching me how to do things that I didn't think would ever come up. One day I felt that I had had enough and I walked out of the class. Rogers followed me out.

"Are you taking off?"

"Yes. I thought I would go to Washington, D.C. and see the nation's capital. I've never been there."

"Do you want me to go with you?"

"No. I am going to take Lyba McPherin if she'll go."

Lyba and I went to Arlington and stayed with my cousin Betty and her husband, Capt. Harold Lamb. They welcomed us with open arms. Harold called a friend for a ride and left us his car. We spent three days looking at the famous monuments and buildings. I was impressed and inspired. At dinner on the third day, Harold said to me, "How long is your leave?"

Lyba said, "What leave? He doesn't have any leave. Do you, Dave?"

I didn't say anything. Harold Lamb looked like he was going to explode. "Are you telling me that I have been harboring a deserter in my house? Feeding him and loaning him my car? I hope you are kidding me. This is nothing to kid about."

"Harold, you aren't a deserter until you have been gone thirty days. I wasn't busy down there at Little Creek and I just took a couple days off. No big deal."

"You are leaving here on the first train in the morning. Betty will drive you to the train and I don't want to know anything about it."

I went back to the Amphibious Base the next afternoon and received a note to report to the base commander. He asked me why I hadn't been attending classes. I told him and he made it very clear I wasn't to do that again.

June 20, 1944

Dear Thorne —

I received your very welcome letter today. I am going to be the skipper of a swell new ship and I am going to have all the responsibility and hard work that I wanted, but I didn't expect them to throw it at me all at once. I had lots of plans as to how I was going to get reacquainted with myself and my friends during the breather spell before I went back to sea and serious work. There wasn't any breather spell. As far as social life is concerned, I would be better off in the South Pacific than here. Time has fallen down a well. When I sit in class, I don't look at my watch and look forward to when the class is over, because when it is over, there is another class waiting for me. I don't count the hours in the day, because tomorrow is just like today.

If any breaks in the routine occur, I will sure let you know, because if I can get away from this world for just a few days, I would like to see you. I would like to spend an evening with you when I didn't have to sit up until the birds were chirping and burping and eating dirty worms in order to be alone with you. You have always seemed to me like a person I would like to know. For I, too, have carried hazy, idealistic pictures around for too long a time.

As Ever,
Love, Dave

July 6, 1944

Dear Mother and Dad,

I have been at sea for a week now, I believe. To tell you the truth, I have rather lost track of time. The training at sea was not such a relaxation as I thought it would be, because they gave us a number of problems in navigation which had to be handed in at the end of the first week. The navigation instructor was an ex-chief quartermaster of a mine sweeper that used to hang around Tulagi, and the minute that he was introduced to me, he said, "You're not the 'Wavey Davey' that hit that sub chaser just off Savo, are you?" From then on, I had a lot of assistance in navigation, and I finally finished it.

I have one more week on this cruise, and I believe that it will be a little more pleasant for me as the navigation will not be so tough. You were exactly right when you worried about my eyes standing the strain. I was pretty worried about that myself, and I believe they just barely made it. I have never had a chance to get new glasses since I have been here, but I think I will when we get back.

On my return to the base, Ensign E. H. Rogers will join me as my executive officer. Rogers is the fellow I came home with on the merchant ship. He had just made ensign after working his way up from apprentice seaman in four years. I believe I told you the story of how he had flunked out of Annapolis, and instead of going home he had joined the Navy and gotten his commission the hard way. I don't know how capable he is as I have never worked with him, but he is a charming social companion, and I am sure that we will get along swell. He must be a good man, or he wouldn't have gone as far as he has. I have all the experience concerning small boats, landing boats, and practical problems that is necessary, and he has the experience that I lack that concerns the routine and red tape connected with operating a large ship.

Up till now the paperwork on this ship has kind of scared me. There are an awful lot of weekly and monthly reports that have to be sent in to Washington. We have to account for all the food we eat and everything else that we use. There are fifteen or twenty logs that have to be kept. They have more files on this ship than they have in most business offices. There is a yeoman and a storekeeper in the ship's company that are busy all the time. I will turn all this work over to Rogers. The ship's company is constantly being added to as more equipment is added to the ship's allowance list.

I have a boatswain's mate first class who has been in the Navy ten years. I think he will be quite a help to me as most of the men are very green and have never been to sea. His name is Horak, and he looks like Gorski's older brother. When I think of the crew of the "324," it is not hard for me to lapse into a sentimental mood. When we are out of these practice maneuvers, we sometimes see LCTs practicing, and when I think of how we started out, it seems like a long time ago. Some of the problems that they tell us we are going to run into, I smile to myself, and one line of the song we used to sing runs through my mind: "For we've been through it all once before."

I was disappointed that I didn't get more time to play around before I got back in the saddle, but if I have to go back,

I can't think of a better way to go than the captain of an LSM. They asked me yesterday if I wanted to transfer to the regular Navy, and be assured of a job the rest of my life. I declined. When I complete this tour of duty as captain of an LSM, my ambitions in the Navy will have been fulfilled, and I will have to devote myself to other activities, or I will never have time to be a cowboy, a fireman, and a locomotive engineer.

When we heard the news on D-Day, I was listening to a radio with a group of ex-LCT, LCI, and LST skippers, most of whom had come back from Europe. Their ships were in that invasion with other captains on them, and it was pathetic to watch them that day. If you read *Time Magazine*, you probably noticed where it said the H hour was at five o'clock in the morning. Then it said, "However, the LCTs went in at midnight carrying the Rangers." The announcements over the radio were rather sickening to me. They sounded like a soap opera and every minute I expected the announcer to say, "Eat Wheaties and you too can be a commando."

I kept thinking that the boys in France were doing a wonderful job, but the boys who were killed in Sicily and Munda and the islands that didn't even make the papers, were just as dead as the boys who were killed in France. I guess I was just jealous that I wasn't there.

It is very late and I must go to bed.

Love, Dave

July 11, 1944

Dear Mother and Dad,

This is the next to last day of my first training cruise and I have probably been about the only person on board that has enjoyed it. One of the reasons I have enjoyed it is that I have gotten lots of sleep and when I wasn't working, I was sitting around soaking up the beautiful sunshine and salt air. The work was not hard and I enjoyed the exercise. I have gained a little weight and feel better than I have felt in months.

Last night I boxed another officer for the amusement of all on board. I don't know whether I won or not. I rather think I did, but anyway we gave the audience their money's worth and neither of us was hurt. I don't know why it is but all you have to do to gain the friendship of the enlisted men is to engage in a prize fight. Up until now the crew of this ship has been rather surly and unpleasant to all the trainee officers, but I noticed this morning that every enlisted man I passed had a smile and a friendly word for me.

Love, Dave

July 26, 1944

Dear Thorne:

I am leaving in an hour for a two week cruise. When I get back from the cruise, I will stay here from one to four days waiting assignment to a ship that is being built. When they tell me which shipyard it is, I will take my crew and go there. If I get sent to Wilmington, maybe you could visit Ann and Sally in Washington and sort of visit me, too.

You are one of the few people in this world and the only girl I know with whom I feel I can afford to be honest so I am not going to beat around the bush. I have been disappointed in my little visit in this country. I saw my family and relatives and friends and enjoyed it very much. I would have been very disappointed if I hadn't seen them. But, I have been so busy with my obligations and my job that there has been no romance. I am going back to the South Pacific as sure as the sun is going to rise tomorrow and the way things stand now, there is no room for romance on my calendar.

I had a good time on my leave but it went fast and you know the story — there were too many people to talk to. I have had a few dates here, but I might as well have stayed at home in bed. I have been so busy that I just don't have time to go out and look for some girl that I might like. Maybe I am hard to please or something but I have just given up looking. If you were to be where I was for just one week it would be wonderful to know that when my work was done I could go out with a girl that I knew I liked and whose company I enjoy.

I realize that in many circles this would be regarded as a screwball suggestion but I am a peculiar guy and there is nothing extremely normal about you. I just thought that possibly if you had quit your job and if you didn't have your mind made up as to what you were going to do next you might be willing to spend a week of your youth entertaining an old sea captain. If, for any of a thousand reasons this wouldn't work, why, just forget it—and when I get back from this trip to the other side of the world I will come up to Michigan and we will shoot a few ducks.

If I get sent to Houston, I don't know of anyone you could visit. I don't know whether you would have to have someone to visit. In fact, I don't know much.

I won't get your answer to this letter until I get back from this cruise two weeks from today. Anything you have to say will be read with interest.

Love, Dave

When we returned from the last two week training cruise, I received orders to take the officers and crew of the LSM 59 to Houston, Texas and await the completion of the building of the ship. No one seemed to know whether it would take a week or a month. The three married officers, Rogers, Wyker, and Bramley immediately called their wives and told them to meet them at the Rice Hotel in Houston.

I didn't want to be without a girl in the midst of all the social activities. On the other hand, I felt strongly that I did not want to form any kind of a commitment to a girl just before I went to a combat area. I gave the matter a lot of thought and wrote Thorne Gray a letter. I told her that if she wanted to meet me in Houston I would show her the time of her life but there were absolutely no strings attached. When the ship left Houston she could forget whatever happened there. I showed the letter to Rogers and he said no girl in the world would answer that invitation. He didn't know Thorne.

When I walked in the lobby of the Rice Hotel in Houston, she was sitting there. She had been there two days. Rogers, Wykers, and Bramley's wives showed up and everybody got acquainted. After a wonderful week in Houston, the Brown Shipyard announced that they were ready to turn the LSM 59 over to the Navy. With a small audience on an extremely hot day, the USS LSM 59 was duly commissioned in the ship canal. Thorne and the wives were present. Very sweet iced tea and cookies were served. There was no air conditioning and everyone was wringing wet. We said good-by to the ladies that night and the next morning we started down the ship canal to Galveston. In Galveston, we outfitted the ship and had our two-week shakedown cruise.

September 4, 1944

Dear Mother and Dad:

I held my first Captain's Mast this morning and awarded the following punishments: Klink and Fiorrentino got five days bread and water in the brig. O'Grady lost the next ten liberties (that should take care of him for a long time), and Timothy lost the next five liberties. I hope that I don't have to do this very often as we don't have our own brig and we have to borrow space in somebody else's. I think the little bit of discipline ought to set the men straight as to what my reaction is when they break my rules. It is going to be different from my LCT. I can't control this big a crew by the strength of my own personality.

As regards the women situation, when I left Lyba in Norfolk, I told her that unless the Navy sent me back there, I would probably never return to Norfolk. I liked Lyba a lot but she isn't the girl I want to marry, and so there is no point in having her sitting around waiting for me. I told Thorne Gray if she wanted to come to Texas to have a good time to come ahead. She came and when she got here I told her not to get any silly ideas in her head because I wouldn't marry her if she were Dorothy Lamour and Betty Grable rolled into one. We had a good time and she left. I told her very distinctly that I wasn't in the right frame of mind to get married and I didn't know when I would be. So that squares her away.

I got a letter from Nancy Goodman today and she said she was getting married on the first of October, so that takes care of her. In other words, I am not leading anybody on.

Love, Dave

September 8, 1944

Dear Mother and Dad,

We have been sitting still for the last few days while we make some necessary repairs on the engines before starting on the last week of the shakedown. The life has been easy for me, as Rogers has been doing all the work. Once I get up in the morning and get the other officers started, I can kind of relax. However, I found out yesterday morning that if I don't get up in the morning, nobody else does. Instead of getting up at six as I usually do, I got up at seven and was astounded to find the decks hadn't been swept down, nobody had eaten breakfast, and everyone was snoring peacefully. I will have to correct this situation.

Love, Dave

Through the Panama Canal

Immediately after we anchored in the harbor at the north end of the Panama Canal, a Naval officer came aboard to give us the word. He said we would start through the canal the next morning at nine o'clock. In the meantime, we could let half of our crew go on liberty at a time. He explained there were two towns here. One that the Americans who operated the canal lived in, and Colon where the natives lived. He said Colon was a horrible place and that is where the sailors would all go. He said that in Colon we must travel in groups of at least three, preferably more. He said if there was any fighting, the men would be arrested and put in jail. Relations with Panama were such that there was nothing that we could do to get them out. The ship would have to sail without them. It sounded very scary.

I gave a lecture to the crew and then turned half of them loose. I went ashore with Rogers and Bramley. It was a very foreign city. One block off the main drag, there was a whole street where girls were selling sex like the boardwalk at the State Fair. It looked to me like sex was the main business in the whole city.

We lost one man in Colon. He was a pharmacist's mate first class. He was the closest thing we had to a doctor on our ship. While he was in bed with some beautiful girl from Guatemala, somebody emptied his pockets. He objected and got thrown in jail. The Navy said that if and when he got out, they would try to send him to us.

We spent the next day going through the Canal. It is very interesting. I had seen a movie a couple years before where Madeline Carroll had been going through the Canal on a pleasure boat and met Fred MacMurray who was a Marine guard. A romance ensued. I imagined myself in some such situation but I couldn't think of anything more romantic than going through the Canal as the captain of my own ship on the way to the South Seas.

It was just before sunset when we got to the Pacific end of the Canal. The Pacific was just as flat as soup on a platter. All the way from Galveston to the Atlantic end of the Canal, the sea had been very rough and the wind never stopped blowing. I had been telling my sick crew that the Pacific wasn't like this. When we got our first view of the flat beautiful Pacific Ocean, the morale went up one hundred percent. Rogers had our course figured and we headed right out into the sunset.

About Face

When we left the Panama Canal, October '44, we sailed on a smooth Pacific Ocean on our way to Bora Bora for about twenty-four hours. In the afternoon of the second day, the fire alarm went off while I was sitting on the john. When I came out of the hatch onto the main deck, I saw smoke pouring out of the hatchway on the starboard side aft. This hatchway was right next to the ammunition locker. We soon had the fire out. When the mess had been cleaned up, Wyker reported that the automatic brake on the shaft had been ruined, and he couldn't tell whether the shaft was permanently damaged or not. I got on the radio and reported this news to the Navy. In about an hour, we received a change of orders. "Report to the destroyer base in San Diego for repairs." We changed course and headed for San Diego.

We found San Diego, successfully entered the harbor, tied up and reported to the office of the commandant. I was told it would take two or three weeks to repair our ship. I could give forty-eight-hour passes to two thirds of the crew at a time, but the captain could not leave the ship for more than eight hours at a time. Rogers immediately called his wife, Blair, and told her to come. Bramley and Wyker decided they couldn't afford it. I enjoyed the many bars of San Diego.

It turned out that going into the repair base at San Diego had really opened a can of worms for our ship. It seems that in the short time since our LSM had been built, the Navy had incorporated several changes in LSMs. So these repairs were made to the LSM 59 while it was in the repair yard of the destroyer base. There were now workmen all over the ship. I was ready to depart San Diego and get on with the war.

Nov. 13, 1944

Dear Mother and Dad:

I am through with the operations now and they are trying to remodel the ship at the last minute. I now have a crew of fifty-five men and five officers. The ship is so torn up from men working on it I can't find a place to sit down. There are about twenty jobs going on at once and about twenty more that should be going on if we are going to be ready on time. Many of the things we want are not easily obtainable and require a lot of following through. We wanted one of these big radios that will pick up all the stations in the U.S. when you are far away and still not give away your position. They are very expensive and hard to get, but we got one with three speakers. We finally got it installed with a speaker in each living compartment. The guys that installed it stole the tubes out of the speakers as they are practically impossible to obtain outside the Navy. I got the tubes back today. We had quite a bit of welding we wanted done in some of the fuel tanks. It is a big job to get the tanks clean enough after you get the fuel out to weld in them.

I would tell you that it is cold and nasty out here, but the weather is a military secret. I think they are protecting the California Chamber of Commerce. Yes, I have needed my heavy blue uniform many times. No, I didn't send for it because every day I thought was going to be my last one here. It is too late now. I will just keep on freezing. Well, when we ran out of syrup for the pancakes, that was the last straw and I decided to take a vacation.

November 14, 1944

Dear Mother and Dad,

I made full lieutenant. I am getting ready to cross that largest body of water in the world again, and I have that feeling of stepping through a door into the unknown. I am not a green ensign this time, and I have a bigger ship, with all that means, but it is still a big step. I expect to see much more interesting country this time. Although I have told you of some of the little things that bother me, and it might sound kind of tough, that is just my way of covering up the enthusiasm I feel for the "adventure" that lies ahead. I really am in good shape, and when the day comes to sail, the LSM 59 will be ready.

I don't have the contact with my men that I had on my LCT, but I am slowly winning them over. When I talk to the men, I tell them what a hero Rogers was in the South Pacific, and when he talks to them, he tells them what a hero I was.

You will certainly have to get over that idea that when I don't write, things are going bad. You will worry yourself to death if you keep that attitude. Always remember that no news is good news.

Mother asked in one of her letters if I lived on my boat. I have never slept anywhere since August 23 except on my boat, except for my trip to Long Beach. I have seldom been ashore. And, Mother dear, this is not a boat. This is a ship. I will get a picture of it someday. It is against the law now.

Love, Dave

Thursday, November 23, 1944

Dear Mother and Dad:

I ought to be in bed tonight, but you have been so much in my thoughts on this Thanksgiving Day that I couldn't pass up the opportunity to drop you a note.

I couldn't help but think on this Thanksgiving Day how very much our family has to be thankful for. During my thirty-three months in the Navy, through living with others and reading their mail, I have become very acutely aware of the continual state of anguish which is the lot of the majority of the common people. There is a steady influx of messages concerning sickness and death, discouragement and despair, death and dishonor. When I grow deathly tired of the misery and sordidness of their cramped lives, all I have to do to bring the sunshine back is to think of my own home and family. And then I realize why I am the captain of the ship while fellows older and stronger than I am swab the deck.

I used to wonder if there was a wall that separated the Country Club District of Kansas City from the rest of the world and kept out unhappiness. But the older I get the more I think the wall is just around our own house and wherever we went we would carry that wall with us. There is no doubt in my mind but that when the war is over we will all spend many Thanksgiving evenings in front of the fireplace recovering from eating too much turkey. And because of this, I have no choice on this Thanksgiving night but to give thanks to the Lord for being a member of a family on which the sun has always shone so brightly.

Whenever I feel so mellow as I do tonight I always think that from now on I will obey all the rules and regulations set down for commanding officers of LSMs. So I better go right down and read all that official mail that has been accumulating on my desk and find out what I have been doing wrong lately.

Love, Dave

Southwest High School in Kansas City, MO was noted for its excellence in education. Built in 1925, it closed in 1998. There are plans to re-open the school in the fall of 2007. "Sachem," the Southwest High School Yearbook of 1936, shows a youthful Davey. The annual stated, "Besides being a member of Baconian, Hi-Y, and Powwow, DAVID CHARLES HAWLEY was a representative of Student Council, a collector on the Trail business staff, and a member of the Senior Business Committee."

The original crew of LCT 324 was pictured in the Saturday Evening Post, *November 3, 1945.*

The caption from this Saturday Evening Post *photo reads: "LCT 324 of the 'Working Navy' at anchor in the Solomons in 1943. Neither captain nor crew could boast of much comfort, but knew they did vital work."*

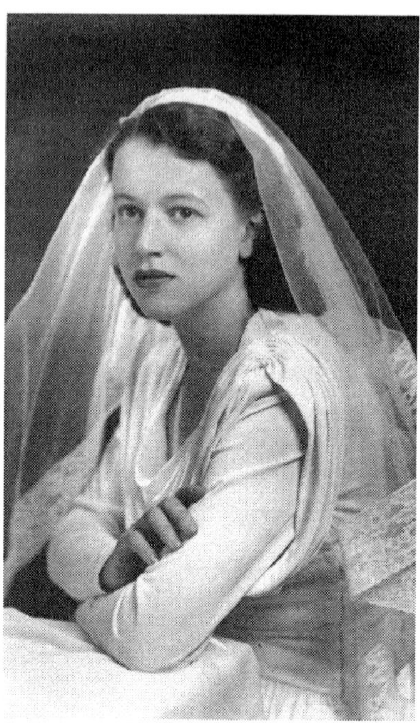

David and Thorne Hawley were married after a week-long engagement in 1945.

The newlyweds enjoyed a leisurely moment together during Davey's military leave.

Davey ran the Ford dealership in Warsaw, Missouri in 1955 while he and Thorne waited for their fourth child, George.

Thorne and the four Hawley children sat for this portrait in the late 1950s.

CHAPTER 4
MORE ACTION

To Pearl Harbor

On November 22, 1944 our orders finally came to depart San Diego and proceed to Pearl Harbor, where we were to report to the commander of Task Force 51.2. I found it is quite a good distance to Hawaii, but the ship and crew went like clockwork. It was a thrill to enter the famous Pearl Harbor that I had heard so much about. There was a whole nest of LSMs just like ours. We anchored near them and began to get acquainted. I met Commander Lind, my squadron leader.

There were liberty boats beginning at ten a.m. and the crew wanted to see the sights. I wanted to go to the officers club and see how many LSM skippers I knew. I found a lot of my old friends there. We went outside of Pearl Harbor a couple times during the next two weeks and had target practice; we shot at targets that were towed by drones. Other than that, we didn't have much to do. I spent most of my time at the officer's club.

December 30, 1944

Dear Mother and Dad,

I received Dad's letter of December 27 today, telling of your Christmas. It goes without saying that I am sorry I wasn't there.

I have been ashore a very few times. I have had many things to do on my ship to get it ready for its future life. Thorne wouldn't recognize the ship she watched getting commissioned. It is a warship now.

I called up Lillian "Lig" Lowry, who was Thorne's roommate at Vassar, and went out there for dinner. She lives in a lovely house with all that goes with it in a place like this. She and her mother were all that were present for dinner, as the father was in the hospital, and the boys are all in the service. The atmosphere was a little stiff for a sea captain who swears at the top of his lungs all day, but I made it. If I have the opportunity, I will accept their invitation to return some night, just for the novelty of going someplace where the people have manners. However, all servicemen have to be off the streets at ten p.m., and it is so far it makes it rather an effort.

Christmas Day we were in port, and there was very little Yuletide spirit shown. I had made up my mind to go ashore, and forget about the Navy, if possible. About five o'clock in the afternoon, I went on deck, and the sight was very depressing. There were about fifty men sitting around, looking very homesick, with no form of recreation, and very little conversation. Enlisted men cannot be ashore here after six p.m., so you see there was not even a beer joint for them to go to. I went below and my conscience bothered me so much that I looked up Rogers and told him we were going to have a party. He looked at me as though I was crazy and said, "What are you going to do — bob for apples?" I thought that was a starter, so I had the cook bring a big tub of water out on deck with two apples. I made Rogers (much against his will) bob with me. Well, in less time than it takes to tell, we had tubs of water all over that deck, and fellows from eighteen to forty years-old bobbing for apples. Then we got a big bowl of corn flakes and water. We took one man from each division, blindfolded him, gave him a spoon, and told him to feed each of the others who was blindfolded. It was a riot. When I got the sheet off my bed and said we were going to play pin the tail on the donkey, I had trouble keeping anyone on watch in the engine room. We have a fellow named Donnelly who was a professional magician before he was drafted, and after we ran out of games, he put on a show for us that was very good. We ended up by singing Christmas carols for about an hour. These fellows pretend to be awfully tough, but it is amazing how much fun they get out of kids games. I forgot to mention that just before the singing, the cook brought out several trays full of food. It was the same stuff they eat every day, but since it was a party, and not regular hour to eat, they devoured it.

Before long, you will be able to keep track of where I am be reading the papers, but for the time being I am as safe as if I was ice skating on Ward Parkway.

I really should mention the Christmas presents I received, but frankly I don't remember who sent me what. The only present that made a big impression was from the Upjohns. They sent me a box and when I opened it, I found its sole content was two boxes of pills. I guess you spoiled me when I was young. I keep opening the boxes looking for a pair of ice skates or an electric train.

Love, Dave

Saipan

Right after Christmas, we were loaded with the equipment we were to carry on the invasion. We carried five tanks, an armored Jeep, sixty-five enlisted Marines and two Marine officers. The Marines were to live on the LSM 59 until they were unloaded on the invasion beach. We had a troop compartment that was designed for this purpose. We were then ordered to proceed to the neighboring island of Maui to practice unloading our tanks. Somebody must have gotten the word that we were going to make this landing at night. We practiced most of the landings in the dark. The Marines would have the tanks fired up before we started our run for the beach. We would open the bow doors, lower the ramp and the tanks would drive off along with the Marines hitting the beach. The more we did it, the faster we got. When the last Marine stepped off the ramp, we would start backing off.

Bramley was on the bridge with me. He was the gunnery officer and in that capacity he had a "talker." There was a talker in each gun tub that relayed Bramley's orders. The crew had nicknamed Bramley the Crow, and they all called him this behind his back. Bramley knew this and didn't like it. One night, right after the Marines landed, and we started backing off, Bramley gave some order and out of the darkness up near the bow somebody went "caw, caw, caw." You could hear laughter all over the ship. It took me several nights to find out who did it.

When we left Pearl Harbor for the next leg in our journey, we traveled in a large convoy. At least it was by far the largest convoy I had ever been in. We were given the courses to steer by signal from the squadron leader. We had a certain position in the convoy to keep. The weather was great and I enjoyed it. When we finally stopped and anchored, we were in the harbor at Saipan. We thought we would be there just overnight, but one day after another dragged slowly by.

January 28, 1945

Dear Mother and Dad,

The most important news item is that I lost my fountain pen over the side. I am writing this letter with one of those kind you dip in the bottle, and because of that, this will be a very short letter.

The main subject of debate here, as it is everywhere, I imagine, is the rapid advance of the Russians. As the European war draws to a close, the question is on the lips of every sailor and Marine out here, "How will that influence me? Will the war workers quit their jobs when Germany is beaten? Will they send huge armies and air forces home or out here to help us? Will all the jobs be taken and the Depression already started by the time we get back to civilian life?"

The boatswain's mate, Horak, injured his leg about a week ago, and the pharmacist's mate, Wallenfely, says he has to remain in bed another day. His first assistant, Susnick, who is the boilermaker who was drafted, is a much more capable and energetic man than Horak, and I will put him in charge. This will also cause complications, as the only other coxswain besides Susnick is Fischer, who is very jealous of Susnick. The only other man who is doing a petty officer's job in the deck force is Drahiem. He is a very hard worker and since he spent fifteen years as a sailor on freighters on the Great Lakes, he is skilled at his job. But he is a Communist, who spends his time, when not on duty, delivering lectures. It has become a neurosis with him, and he believes he is being persecuted by being forced into the Navy. I have tried to transfer him, but it is very difficult to explain to some commander of a receiving station that you want to transfer a man because he is a Communist.

Do you realize that I have been gone from home eight months already? When I think about how many years I was gone from home during those two weeks I spent at Camp Gravois in the summer, I can't imagine where those eight months have gone.

Love, Dave

February 8, 1945

Dear Mother and Dad:

My hair is about half an inch long, and no one on board has over an inch of hair. My back is brown and very few shirts are worn these days. Many of the men have been growing beards and it had begun to look like a pirate crew, but the commander of our group who doesn't approve of pirate crews said all faces must be shaved clean. I have had a bad sty on my right eye and I have been wearing a black patch over that eye when I stand on the bridge looking into the sun. Well, if you don't think I looked like the captain of the *Jolly Roger* I wish you would speak to the commander.

The crew hasn't been ashore for a month now and they and the captain are beginning to get a little jumpy. Trouble with some of the men's health is already beginning to crop up as I knew it would. I don't think these older fellows hold up as well as those young fellows like I had on the "324." Fischer, the coxswain with five children, is having so much trouble with his rheumatism and arthritis he can hardly get up and down the ladders. He is only thirty-seven years old but on and off the relief all his life has been a tough fight. It was enough to make a man turn to drink and Fischer finally did. Horak, the boatswain mate, has a sore on his leg that won't heal. I have a hunch that he pulls the scab off every night. The new cook, Julies Ceroli, weighs two hundred and fifty pounds with no muscle on him. When he gets in his bunk at night and the man gets in above him and the man gets below him, he can't roll over. It is beginning to wear on his morale pretty bad. Draheim, the Communist, listens to the Japanese broadcast every night and agrees with everything they say. Short bitter arguments spring up among the crew without a minute's notice all day long, but as long as I hear the monotonous grind of those engines turning over and over, I know it is all right because it is a sure indication that the day is approaching when they won't have time for their petty arguments.

I received Dad's last letter saying where he thought I was and I am afraid that if any of his mail was ever censored, the Navy would not believe that he was just a good guesser.

February 9, 1945

Dear Mother and Dad:

My eye is greatly improved today and I have discarded my black patch. There is practically nothing that I can tell you at present about our present deployment. I can tell you that some of the hours I spend on the bridge, I spend in conversation with Robert Q. Will, one of the signalmen. Will was a professional clam digger in civilian life and he can tell wonderful tales of his experiences as a clam digger. Donnelly, the professional magician, is in his thirties with two kids and was quite a figure in the civilian defense program in New Jersey. He gave lectures on how to put out fires and how to combat gas attacks all along the Eastern sea coast. We really have some characters on this ship.

Rogers expected his baby the first of February so the next time we get mail he expects to receive the news. Wyker's wife is supposed to have her baby the first of March. In my opinion, every one of the four officers I live with is inconsiderate of the others. We live so close together that such things are very noticeable. I have done a lot of thinking about it and I have come to the conclusion that if parents can teach their children the virtues of consideration, patience, tolerance and appreciation, they have done a good job and can forget about the rest.

Love, Dave

February 10, 1945

Dear Mother and Dad:

You know that old saying "No news is good news." I think that must have originated in the Navy, as all the news I ever get is bad. I had a juicy one today. The "oil king" who is the motor machinist who is in charge of all oil and water aboard informed me this morning that during the night someone had opened the wrong valves and pumped nine hundred gallons of lube oil into the ocean. Understand, this isn't fuel oil, it's lube oil, and although nine hundred gallons isn't very much, we had just enough, and now we don't. This will be taken care of somehow, but it is another headache. There is a new one every day.

Love, Dave

Iwo Jima 1945

We finally had our last briefing and were shown the pin point on the map called Iwo Jima where we were going to land our tanks. We proceeded out of the harbor at Saipan and joined a big convoy headed north. Everyone on the ship knew where we were going and what his job was when we got there. We arrived in the Iwo Jima staging area at night of the third day. It was February 18th. Rogers' wife, Blair, was due to have her first child the next day.

Our orders were to be on the line of departure at dawn. It wasn't very rough but you can't sit still with a ship in the ocean unless you are anchored. We had to keep moving. Beginning about four o'clock in the morning, the Marines began playing with the engines in those tanks. When it got light, from my position on the bridge, about forty feet about the water, I could see a long ways. In front of us two miles of open water and then the bleak island. It looked like a small mountain on the north end with high cliffs on the south end with sloping beaches in between. There were several small ships that had been broached on the beach, thus reducing the area where you could get a boat up to the beach. Behind us there were ships as far as I could see. The farthest ships were the big battleships. There were aircraft carriers, cruisers, destroyers, attack transports, and all kind of support vessels. I couldn't help but wonder what the Japanese on the island thought when they looked out that morning and saw what looked like a thousand ships.

I thought the LSMs would land in a big wave all at once, but we didn't. There wasn't enough clear space on that beach for more than three at the most. We sat there and watched some small landing craft go in and land. It didn't look like they were doing any good: it was hard to see. Finally, the first LSMs were ordered in. First one would go in at the north end of the beach and when all the firepower was concentrating on it, one would land at the south end. There was an open place on the beach between two wrecked cargo vessels and that was where they picked for us to land. It was quiet there when we got our order to go in. But as we headed for the beach and got up speed, all hell broke loose in our landing spot. One big geyser of water after another showed where their shells were landing. It was right where we were going to land.

Over the radio came the order, "LSM 59 return to line of departure." I didn't need to hear that twice.

"Hard right rudder." The fact that I had started to turn must not have been obvious to Commander Lind. The next order was more urgent.

"LSM 59 return to line of departure. Dave, come back, come back."

I answered him then. "We are returning to line of departure."

We sat on the line of departure with everyone chewing their fingernails for another half hour. Then, we got the word to try it again. The geysers had stopped going off in our hole. Another LSM had just landed in the hole to the north. It got hit with something that set it afire on its way in. It was burning before it got to the beach. But it got to the beach, opened the bow doors and lowered the ramp. When I saw this, I turned to Bramley and told him to order all gun crews to take cover.

When he looked at me and said, "What do you mean?"

I said, "Tell them to lie down in the gun tubs. Everybody exposed is going to get hit."

We made it to the beach, opened the bow doors and lowered the ramp. I was wearing a combat helmet like everyone else. I was just peeking over the armor plating surrounding the conn. When we lowered the ramp, the first twenty feet of beach was covered with Marines lying there. I grabbed the electric horn and yelled for them to roll out of the way. Rogers was in the bow in charge of the repel boarders party.

He yelled back at me, "These men can't roll. They are all dead."

I looked again and realized that many of them were not dead, but wounded. Two of Rogers' men in the repel boarders party were already bringing in the wounded that were blocking the tanks' way.

There were two men that were voluntarily exposing themselves on the beach as they brought in the wounded, named Will and Noone. I had never seen either one of them work before. Lt. Springer driving the first tank was edging onto the ramp and the Marine warrant officer driving the second tank was right behind him. On either side of the tanks, the wounded were streaming onto the ship. I could hear small arms fire hitting the ship all around me. I watched a mortar shell fired from Surabachi come toward us and it looked like it wasn't coming any faster than a football. It fell thirty yards short and sent up a big geyser of water. Will and Noone had cleared a path wide enough for a tank, but Springer wasn't going. His tank sat on the ramp. I could talk to him by radio and I told him to go.

He said to me, "I think you got the wrong beach, Captain." I was shocked.

"There is only one beach and this is it. Drive it off."

They were shooting a big mortar at us from the south end of the island and this too looked very slow in coming, but it made a gigantic geyser of water. The next shell from Surabachi landed thirty feet closer than the last. They were getting our range.

I told Springer, "Either drive it off or back it on. We can't stay here."

Springer said, "I want to do the right thing. If I am supposed to drive off here I will. But, I think this is the wrong place."

The shell fire from all around us was now being concentrated on our area and it was very bad for the Marines lying on the beach. They were motioning for us to go away. We couldn't go away as long as Springer's tank was sitting on our ramp. We had practiced at Maui until we could unload our tanks and start off the beach in five minutes. Someone said later, it was twenty minutes from the time we hit the beach until Springer drove his tank off. Just as he drove it off, a mortar shell coming from the south landed close enough to our starboard quarter to move the ship over and we on the bridge were drenched with the water from its geyser. Then from the engine room telephone, a message came that the starboard engine had quit running.

When Springer finally drove his tank off, the second tank followed him immediately and quickly passed him, but there was a big gap between the second and third tanks. This gap had become full of wounded Marines from the beach.

When the mortar shell landed so close to our stern, Bramley had taken cover at my feet. He grabbed hold of my pants with both hands, jerked on them, and yelled, "Back her off." Between then and when we finally got off, several more shells landed close enough to jar the ship and cover us with water. Each time, Bramley would jerk on my pants and yell, "They hit us again. Back her off." Rogers was now pointing at the wounded men that filled the bow and saying "What do you want to do with them?" I decided that about one more mortar shell and the decision would be made for us. So I took Bramley's advice and backed her off. I was rather surprised that the one engine would do it. As soon as possible I turned around and went out beyond the line of departure where we could lick our wounds and think. I believe the hardest thing to get used to in a battle is the noise. In getting people ready for an act like this, they never tell them about the noise. It is hard to think with all that noise.

I found a hospital ship that would take the wounded. It wasn't easy because the sea had gotten rougher and we only had one engine. Most of the crew seemed to be in a daze. Horak, the salty boatswain's mate, had hidden himself behind the anchor winch while we were on the beach. Now he seemed to be asleep with his eyes open. It was a lot of work to transfer the wounded. I tried to keep the LSM from banging into the hospital ship while Rogers supervised the few men that seemed capable of working. We found we had eight men who were dead. The hospital ship wouldn't take them. These were men that Will and Noon had moved to let the tanks off. I was getting ready to steam out to sea and put them in mattress sacks when I found somebody that would take them.

Iwo Jima, Day Two

We spent the night of D-Day trying to stay in one spot out of the way. We were safe behind the line of departure. Wyker and his engineers spent the night trying to get our starboard engine to run. We still had most of the Marines on board. We had radio speakers turned up on the main deck so the crew and the Marines could hear the ship-to-shore messages that we were hearing in the radio shack. Very little progress was being made on that beach. Some of the crew had kept their heads down and been well enough hidden so that they hadn't seen the terrible sight on that beach. They were the lucky ones. Of course, they saw the casualties on the ship. But those that had been in the repel boarders party and had helped Will and Noone clear a path for the tanks to drive off were strangely quiet.

We received orders during the night to unload the rest of our tanks and the Marines at dawn. The starboard engine still wasn't running. The mortar that had exploded next to it had broken the oil lines and they hadn't all been repaired yet. Wyker said it would run a few minutes in a pinch if we got stuck on the beach.

We landed that same place we had landed the day before. The beach was still covered with men but they were obviously in better shape than they had been that first day. That first day when we opened the bow doors just to the right of the open bow door lay a Marine who had lost both his hands. He was obviously alive. When we came in on "D Plus One," I couldn't help looking to see if he was still there. He was gone. We got unloaded with no major problems, and got off the beach. By noon, Wyker had the starboard engine running at half speed. It helped a lot in going alongside another ship.

We started picking up Marines off of the APAs, troop carriers, and carrying them into the beach. They sure looked young. Maybe I had grown older in the last couple days. We carried Marines, ammunition and food. The beach was a flurry of activity. On the afternoon of the fourth day, a Marine captain came on my ship while we were unloading on the beach. He wanted to fill two canteens with coffee. He said to me, "No one who hadn't been there would believe how bad it is here."

"When did you get here, Captain?"

"I landed this morning about eight o'clock."

I realized that the Marine who lands on "D Plus Four" will never know what it was like for the Marine who landed on D-Day. Nobody can tell him because he feels he has seen it all.

After D-Day, More Challenges

After an exhausting ten days of carrying Marines and equipment into the beach, we were returning empty for another load when we had an accident. A big square steel pontoon had broken away from a causeway they were trying unsuccessfully to build. A wave caught it and banged the sharp corner into our port side. It cut through the side of the LSM 59 and made a hole under the water line in the engine room a little bigger than a basketball. The water poured in. We were close to a lot of other ships. We weren't going to drown, but if somebody didn't do something, our ship was going to sink right there. The skin of the ship was about three feet from the side of one of the big Fairbanks Morse diesel engines. I was standing there watching that stream of water shoot across that three feet wondering what to do when a sailor touched me on the shoulder and said, "Don't worry, Captain. The ship won't sink. Water seeks its own level. When the water on the inside gets as high as the water on the outside, it will stop coming in." I said, "Why, certainly. Why didn't I think of that?"

Soon the crew were repeating this to one another. It sounded logical and reassuring. In the meantime, Rogers was rigging a collision mat out of a mattress. He had four lines under the ship at the stern, and two lines over the top of the ship. He slid the mattress forward toward the hole. The problem was to find the hole. It was a couple feet below the water line and we couldn't see it. I repelled off the side and, holding onto a line from the deck, I felt with my feet for the hole. When I found the hole, my whole leg went in, and the suction plastered me against the side of the ship. I couldn't get any leverage to pull my leg out. My head was against the side of the ship was above water between waves. While I was in this position, I heard one of the sailors on the deck say, "He has more guts than brains." Somebody finally went to the engine room and shoved my leg out and we got the collision mat over the hole. We didn't sink.

Because of the magnitude of the operations at Iwo Jima, they had every kind of support ship imaginable including a floating dry dock. They towed the LSM 59 into the floating drydock. When they pumped the water out of the drydock, the LSM was high and dry. They pumped the water out of the LSM and welded a plate over the hole. Our ship would now float but it would not run. Our participation in the battle for Iwo Jima was over. They anchored us at the other end of the beach from Surabachi and out far enough so we were in no danger from the Japs. We sat there for another ten days.

Navy ships in 1945 did not have air conditioning, but they had an excellent system of ventilation. I was never aware of how necessary it was until our fans stopped. The bulkheads or walls of the compartments below deck were covered with water. When I tried to get into my bunk, the sheets felt like I could wring them out with my hands. There was no way you could sleep below deck. We had no stoves to cook with and no refrigeration. That pretty well eliminated everything we had been eating. Cold food out of cans was about it. Everyone slept on the deck.

The war on Iwo Jima ended on the cliffs over our heads. We had ringside seats. As we ate our cold green beans out of a can, we watched the dive bombers harass the remaining Japs.

At the end of ten days of this, we received orders that we were to be towed to Saipan by a seagoing tug. We rigged a bridle on our bow and hooked a two-inch wire cable from us to the tug. It is over six hundred miles from Iwo Jima to Saipan and nobody thought it would be easy, but the weather was very rough and very wet and the combination made the conditions unbelievably hard. We were eating unappetizing food in the rain. The sea was so rough that the tug had to proceed slowly. They couldn't keep an even strain on the cable. On the third day, with big waves and lots of rain, the cable parted. As soon as we were loose from the tug, and not making forward progress, our ship turned sideways in the trough of the waves. Then, we really began to roll. I had a small battery-powered radio with which I could talk to the tug. He said he had another cable, but he was afraid to come anywhere close to us. He would come close enough to use his line-throwing gun and we would have to pull the cable over by hand. Our winch, of course, wouldn't work without electricity.

I don't think they had ever used that line-throwing gun before and the first two attempts didn't reach our ship. On the third attempt, the pellet carrying the small line sailed across our ship and the crew caught the line and started pulling it in. Fifty men pulled on the wet and heavy line. Suddenly, it snapped. In the meantime, the wind was blowing us away from the tug. The tug tried to shoot us another line: seventeen times they shot their line across the ship but the wind and rain was against us. Fourteen hours we wallowed and drifted and hauled in on the wet lines. It never stopped raining.

Susnick, the boatswain's mate came up to me and said, "Captain you have to give up now. We can't do this any more. Look at my hands." His hands were just raw. "All the men's are like mine. We can't pull this thing in. We have used up every ounce of strength for this."

The crew gathered round me when they saw I had something to say. I told them the batteries were dead in the radio. The tug captain said this was the last pellet in the line-throwing gun. We were being blown toward Japan and enemy waters.

"This is what we came for. This is it."

But this time we got to get the cable and dropped the eye over the bits. They towed us to Saipan.

We got to Saipan in the evening and I went ashore. The officer I was supposed to report to was afloat. "You will have to wait until tomorrow to see him."

I asked, "How will I get back to my ship?"

They had a boat pool downstairs. I went to the boat pool officer and asked to get back to my ship. He was a lieutenant and said, "If you guys don't think we have anything to do but run a taxi service for officers who want to have a drink, you're wrong. The trouble with you fellows is that you come from San Pedro where you have small boats run for everything you want, a stamp to mail a letter to your mother. You think that all we are here for is a taxi service. These boats are for business, not for pleasure."

I hadn't eaten for a day and a half, and I hadn't been to bed for so long I couldn't remember. I was terribly tired. I stood looking at him and I thought, "If the Marine captain who lands on 'D Plus Four' can't understand what it was like on D-Day, how can I expect this poor fellow who sits behind a desk on Saipan to understand. It is not my job to educate him."

I turned on my heel and walked out. I asked a coxswain from an APA to take me back to my ship. He said he would be glad to. My men were lying on the deck all wet, tired, hungry, and beaten to nothing. I started laughing at them and they asked, "What's the matter?" I said, "The boat pool officer thinks we are a bunch of draft dodgers."

The next day, a team of experts thoroughly inspected LSM 59 and finally decided it was worth repairing. It was a big job. The engine room had been completely flooded with salt water and all the electric motors and everything of an electrical nature had to be rebuilt. It took a month and a half. By the time the LSM 59 was ready for sea, the remnant of my LSM Flotilla was gone. We were alone.

March 7, 1945

Dear Mother and Dad,

I was happy to hear that brother Georgie may get a chance to finish his college education before going on active duty. I know that these boys resent going to school at a time like this, but it is my opinion that these ensigns they are turning out today, who have not graduated from college, and who have never worked, are too young for the job they are supposed to do. Spud Casson, the young officer on my ship, is too young and inexperienced for this job. I have given him hell so much for some of the dumb things he has done, and the whole life today is such a drastic change for him, that he becomes very low in spirits sometimes. I have even considered evacuating him. By the way, I evacuated Horak, the boatswain's mate, and also Drahiem, the Communist. Horak was just plain yellow, and made himself sick with fright. Drahiem wasn't yellow, be he didn't have the guts to put up with the living conditions. I have Sisswick as my boatswain's mate now, and he does a good job. I had had several differences with Rogers, while the going was smooth, but when the going got rough, Rogers really went to work, and we made a good team. Rogers really did the job of the BM.

I don't hear the same war news that you hear, but I would caution you not to be too optimistic. The war gets tougher as we get closer to Japan. These Japs just don't surrender when they are licked. They fight to the last man.

I had to back down to keep from hitting an LCI gunboat one night, and when I cussed them out over my electric bull horn, a voice came back saying, "Dave, is that you?" It was Harry Smith. He is now the captain of his own LCI.

I have taken quite an interest in watching the reactions of the strain on some of the other commanding officers. One thing that many people don't realize is that it takes two different kinds of courage to fight a war. One kind is the kind it takes to stand up and do your job when you are being shot at. The other kind of courage is the kind it takes to keep going day after day when you aren't being shot at. When the hours are long, the work is hard, and the living conditions get worse day after day, it takes a lot of courage to keep on doing your best. That is when it takes good steady driving officers.

Among other things, the washing machine is gone now, and I am back to washing my own clothes. I spent two hours this morning getting the grease out of a pair of pants. Then I hung them up on the life line and they blew over the side and were lost. The crew thought this very funny.

Love, Dave

March 12, 1945

Dear Mother and Dad:

When will this ship stop rollin' and pitchin'? Well, I'll tell you, never. You might as well say goodbye to your stomach when you go to sea. I was thinking last night when I was helping Susnick and Rogers wrestle some four-by-fours in between the towing bridle and the bow, how many hours are wasted by foolish boys dreaming of how they would like to go to sea. So the doctor said a sea voyage with salt air would do the patient good. Did you ever try sleeping in a dungeon where there had been no light or ventilation for days? Sure, the captain says you can put a cot out on the deck, but you better tie it down or it will slide all over the deck. After you get in it, be sure and have somebody tie the blankets on you or they will blow off as soon as you let go of them. Then, after you make up your mind you are going to stick it out it starts to rain.

March 13, 1945

Dear Mother and Dad:

I can stand the bullets and the noise, the explosions and sudden death, but this slow death by rolling and pitching and hanging a man's stomach around his ears is enough to take the fight out of Samson. There must be a line somewhere about "With a crew half mad, and foully clad."

In four days, Rogers' six-year enlistment will be up. Rogers is undoubtedly a father by now, but goodness knows when he will ever hear whether it is a boy or a girl.

The Navy has a new rule on censoring which says you can tell where you have been a month after you leave. Therefore, if you are interested, I could tell you I have been to Eniewetock. I have also paid my respects to Saipan.

I was thinking the other night when my troubles seemed to be unending how I could possibly be worse off. It took a long time but I finally got the answer. I could have been standing on the beach when my ship sailed over the horizon without me. In that way I would have missed all this and I would never have been satisfied as to what it was like.

Love, Dave

March 16, 1945

Dear Mother and Dad,

Yesterday, the wounded lady with her crew of weary fighting men pulled into calm waters and let the ribbon clerks and landlubbers stare at her. My commanding officer was waiting for me with a warm handclasp, and took me immediately to the officers club, where he began to ply me with beer so the saga of the sea would flow freely. I hadn't seen him to talk to in six weeks, and I didn't know what his reaction to our troubles had been. I was relieved to find he had nothing but praise for the Fighting Fifty-Nine. As the cold beer ran down my throat in the atmosphere of warm friendship, and I looked out the window and saw the Fifty-Nine resting in the calm water, my troubles began to slide off my shoulders. I guess the world can still be a pleasant place even for a sailor.

Love, Dave

March 29, 1945

Dear Mother and Dad,

It is quite a mystery to me why you are so thoroughly convinced that I didn't take part in the invasion of Iwo Jima. There are two different newsreels being shown in the U.S. today, which show the LSM 59 on the beach at Iwo Jima. Several members of the crew have received letters from their families saying they saw us clearly. However, Bramley's wife has been going to the newsreels constantly and hasn't seen us. She also was a doubting Thomas, but she sent us the enclosed clipping, so I guess she is convinced now. Maybe this clipping will even convince you. We carried this correspondent on D Plus Four, and he was so badly scared, he misquoted me. Next time I carry a correspondent, I will treat him more graciously.

We are still licking our wounds, so if they have any excitement in the Pacific in the next couple of weeks, you can rest assured I ain't there.

Rogers and Wyker are both fathers of baby boys. They try to take their new responsibility very seriously, but they don't get much cooperation.

You asked me about a barber. We have two barbers, with all the equipment. One of them is an Indian who cut everybody's hair on the reservation. The other is the father of seven children and from cutting their hair branched out to the neighborhood children.

The colored steward's mate washes my clothes, or at least he did, but after Iwo, the washing machine would require a major operation before it would wash anything. I have taken to my old habit of getting new clothes from time to time and throwing my dirty ones over the side.

If you still don't believe I was at Iwo Jima, on the next invasion, I will box up a Jap and send him home. Enough of this drivel.

Love to all, Dave

Easter morning, 1945

Dear Mother and Dad,

It's a bright clear Easter morning in the Pacific. About once an hour, it starts to rain. It rains very heavily for about five minutes, and then it stops just as abruptly as it started. The sun shines even while it rains. I have on my Easter suit, of which I am very proud. Joe Duckett finally got around to washing all of my clothes, and when I got in the small boat to start for church on the beach, my clothes were nice, clean, faded khakis.

Last night, I told the crew I would take all the men ashore today who wanted to go to church. This morning about twenty men were ready to go. I asked them at the gangway to divide into two groups — those going to the Catholic services and those going to the Protestant. I was surprised and disappointed to find I was the only one on the Protestant side of the line.

I was sorry that I didn't send Mother a corsage for Easter, but I have not been able to get a money order for two months — even if I had any money.

I have a lot of time to spend reading books, and I enjoy that very much. I just finished W. Somerset Maugham's *Of Human Bondage* and I considered it a great waste of time. I feel certain that I could write a better book than this.

The news from Europe is very good, and we have high hopes that it won't be too long now before that vast army over there starts coming over here.

Did you read in the *Reader's Digest* about the island in the South Pacific where the Navy commander issued shirts to the native women? They hadn't been in the habit of wearing anything above the waist, and it disconcerted his men. The women wore the shirts, but they cut two holes in the front of them for comfort.

I read in *Time* magazine that the good war news in Europe had been paid for the stock market, so I guess I am not as wealthy as I was last week.

Love, Dave

April 18, 1945

Dear Mother and Dad:

I am still becalmed and growing more restless every day, but it can't last forever. When we are in port like this, after I make the first few arrangements when we arrive, there is really nothing for me to do. A very welcome diversion was *Captain Horatio Hornblower*. I hate to admit that I have had that book on my shelf over my bed all this time and never opened the front page. However, I was so fed up with the sea and the Navy by the time I got a minute to read, that I wanted to read about something entirely foreign from what I was doing. About a week ago, I picked that book up, and I couldn't lay it down. I read with *Knight's Seamanship* (the sea-going man's Bible) at my elbow, and looked up every term that I didn't know. After I had read about one third of it, Rogers, who had been listening to me talk about it, couldn't resist it, and we read it together.

We diagrammed on paper every battle he was in, we erected the jury masts in miniature, and we had every compartment and every sail on his ship drawn in. It was the first sea story I ever read that sounded real. Rogers and I enjoyed the book immensely, and if you find it convenient, maybe you could send me *Captain from Connecticut*. We have already discovered that *Commodore Hornblower* is running in the *Saturday Evening Post*, so it won't be necessary to send me that.

The other afternoon, I was in the officers' club on the beach, and the colored steward's mates were sweating to sell the beer as fast as several hundred officers drank it. Some Seabees had been digging a big deluxe privy out in back when I came by. They evidently got tired of digging in that hard coral, and decided to blast a little hole. Suddenly, from right behind this frame building that serves as the club, came a loud explosion, and rocks began to rain on its tin roof. Three out of four officers in that club, including the steward's mates, hit the deck instantly. As I picked myself up off the floor, I realized that those fellows on the floor, including the steward's mates, were off of ships that knew enough to duck the flying shrapnel, and those sitting up were land-based members of the Naval base.

Love, Dave

April 30, 1945

Dear Mother and Dad,

I have time only for a note. At last she runs, and they didn't waste any time putting me back to work. The whole crew is glad to get moving again, and I know that I am the happiest of all. I have tried hard to keep the men busy during this period of inactivity, and it is a relief to me to have them so tired from standing sea watch that all they want to do is sleep.

Under Sisswick, the watches move much smoother than they did under Horak, and after their experience at Iwo Jima, the crew is easier to handle. Wish me luck, but don't worry about me. I have already encountered about every emergency that could arise down here, and nothing worries me. I feel as though I were starting Chapter Two in the second volume of "Wavey Davey's Adventures In the Saga of Men Against the Sea."

All my love, Dave

June 4, 1945

Dear Mother and Dad,

It was funny about me getting the wrong Sunday for Mother's Day. I called the crew to quarters that Sunday, and announced that it was Mother's Day, and that I wanted every man on board to write to his mother. We knocked off all work while they wrote their letters, and now I find out it was the wrong week.

I enjoyed Mother's letter, with its description of Fulton, Missouri very much. There is no one who can describe a town or person in fewer words, give as emphatic and candid a picture, as Mother. She knows what she likes and dislikes! There is something about her letters that make me feel like she is sitting in the room talking to me. After reading one, if I started to do something of which she would not approve, I would feel as self-conscious as if she were standing there watching me.

You know, it is a funny thing. Since I have been in the Navy, I have been in many a midnight bull session with brother officers who described their home life through the rigors of grade school and high school. I have never found anyone who spent those years as pleasantly as I did. I remember once in Michigan, somebody said, "The Hawley children weren't raised. They grew up by themselves." I know now that this is entirely false, because I believe I have met no other boys who have instilled in them as deeply the beliefs and principles of their parents.

Maybe I am a little tired of the rain and the general quarters, and am a little homesick tonight, but it sounds good to hear Mother give somebody hell.

Love, Dave

Okinawa

When they rebuilt my ship at Saipan, they built an airplane cockpit on one end of the bridge. There was a seat for the pilot and controls for flying a small plane. The ship was equipped with a radio that was designed to fly drones or pilotless planes. A Navy pilot named Lt. Thompson was assigned to our ship's company. It was his job to sit in the little cockpit and fly the drones or whatever use the radio was put to. He didn't know anymore than we did. Surprisingly, he was delighted to be assigned to our ship. He said it would give him a chance to see the war firsthand and that is what he wanted. The rest of the officers cringed when he told how he looked forward to combat.

We went to the island of Ulithi and picked up a shipment of drones and then proceeded to Okinawa where the war was going on. I reported to the staff gunnery officer under Admiral Hill. He said the Jap Kamikaze or suicide planes were coming in every night flying over the heads of the anti-aircraft gunners on the ships on the picket line. We were to fly some drones past the picket line and see if they could hit them. We did this for a few days and it was fun. Then, they sent for me on the admiral's flag ship.

When I appeared on the flagship for my orders, the gunnery officer explained. "As you know, we are losing a lot of ships to suicide planes. At Kama Retto we have a harbor full of ships that have been damaged beyond repair but are still afloat. The admiral thinks that these ships strategically located could attract some of the suicide planes. One of these ships is the *USS Barry*, a destroyer escort. We want you to take the *Barry*, equip her with lights you can turn on with your fancy radio that was designed to fly drones. You also should have some fifty caliber machine guns loaded with tracers that you can turn on with your radio. I think a smoke pot in the stack would be a good idea, too. We will furnish the technicians to install these things and hook them up to your radio. After we get the Barry ready, you are to tow her out beyond the picket line and set her up where the Japanese suicide planes can't miss seeing her. You will then remove yourself to a safe distance. When you see the Japanese planes coming, you will turn on enough lights and fire enough tracers to make sure the Japs see her. Hopefully, the Jap planes will sink her by crashing into her."

Two days later, on the afternoon of June 21st, 1945, we steamed out of Kama Retto with the disabled *USS Barry* in tow. The admiral's staff had furnished us with sixteen technicians who had rigged the lights and the guns and the smoke pots on the *Barry* that we could control with our radio. Four of the technicians were still on the *Barry* putting finishing touches to their work. The rest of the technicians were on the LSM 59 where they were either working on the controls or leaning on the rail wondering where we were going.

The gunnery officer from the admiral's staff was standing on the bridge beside me. It was easy to look at a chart and figure the most direct compass reading to Japan. That is the way we were headed.

Around Okinawa there was line of destroyers, destroyer escorts, and other war ships that was called the "picket line." Their purpose was to stop the suicide planes before they got to the big ships in the harbor. Their success had been limited. We passed through the picket line and headed toward Japan. From my position on the bridge, I could talk through the speaking tube to the wheelhouse below me or I could listen to some of their conversation through the same tube. Through this tube, I heard a signalman in the wheelhouse ask Susnick, our boatswain mate, why he was wearing his life jacket. Susnick finally said, "I am wearing my life jacket because the Captain is wearing his life jacket. The Captain knows where we are going. I don't. If he is going to wear his jacket, I think I will wear mine." Sailors hated to wear those warm life jackets, but everybody started putting them on.

When we got out of sight of the picket line, I stopped to take the technicians off of the *Barry*. We were having the evening chow a little early. We had removed the towing cable and I was getting ready to go alongside the *Barry*. Then the Jap planes arrived. Instead of flying way overhead where I expected them, they were flying just a few feet over the water. When they fly low like that, at four hundred miles per hour, they come over the horizon and are on you before you can say "general quarters." The first one hit the *Barry* and there was a tremendous explosion and a large fire started. I headed for the *Barry* to get the four technicians. Suddenly, there was a Jap plane right beside me. I could see the pilot. Then, we were hit. He crashed into the well deck about two thirds of the way back. It was right over the engine room. Explosion, fire and thick smoke. On a ship like the LSM 59 almost all orders were given over the PA system. When I realized it was dead, I had a momentary feeling of helplessness.

Most of the crew were eating supper in the bow of the ship and were not hurt in the explosion. The smoke which rose up right behind the conning tower, cut off my vision of the stern and I couldn't see what was happening back there. We obviously had a bad fire. The ship was dead in the water. I stared down to see how bad the damage was but the wheelhouse was as far as I could get as the flag deck was on fire. On either side of the ship, there was a built-in compartment of CO2 with a long hose and big nozzle. I managed to get to the one on the starboard side and I turned the powerful nozzle on the fire. Almost immediately, the hose from the port side was in use beside me. I knew without looking, that that hose was manned by Ed Rogers. When we blew the fire and smoke back with our powerful nozzles, we could see a gigantic hole in the deck. Then there was someone beside me saying, "I'll take that hose, Captain." Rogers and I were both relieved from our hose duty by seamen Noone and Will. They were the same guys that cleared the beach of wounded at Iwo Jima. It flashed through my mind, I haven't seen those guys since Iwo. They've been doping off somewhere. I said to Rogers, "Abandon ship. You take the starboard side, and I'll take the port side."

We had had so many abandon ship drills on the "59," the crew had begun to think I was crazy. It paid off. Everybody did their job. The rafts were launched after the muster was taken at each raft. There had been two men killed in the engine room when the plane hit. There had been several men burned. The ship was sinking rapidly by the stern. The bow was sticking up in the air out of the water. I had two technicians left on my side when Rogers called, "The starboard side is all clear."

When the stern went down, the bow went straight up. I was in the water in front of the ship! The bow was sticking up over my head. I was swimming as hard as I could but the suction was keeping me from getting away from the ship. The bow was coming over on top of me; it was falling in front of me. The ship was going down. It seemed like I went down and down and down. Suddenly, I was going up. I had on my kapok life jacket and it felt like I went clear out of the water when I hit the surface. I looked around and I was alone, but I was alive. The ship was gone. I had a tremendous feeling of relief. I did my job till the end. It was over for me. I didn't care what happened now.

I had all my clothes on including my shoes. I discovered that I still had my hat on. It was pulled way down over my forehead, but I still had it on. The water was a moderate temperature. The waves were too high for me to see other people in the water. I couldn't see our rafts. The buoyancy of the salt water and my kapok life jacket made me float easily with no effort, but I was isolated. There was nothing I could do for my ship or its crew.

I knew from the charts that the Pacific Ocean is over a mile deep at this spot. How long will it take the ship to sink to the bottom? I knew I would be picked up. A lot of people, including the admiral, knew I was out here.

After drifting isolated for quite a while, the waves washed me into the same trough with two other survivors of my crew. One had been badly burned on his back and had no life jacket. We got the wounded man between us. He was semi-conscious and easy to deal with. These two men were greatly relieved to find me, especially when I told them I was absolutely certain that we would be picked up as soon as it got light.

"Half of the Navy will be out here looking for us."

We watched the sky light up when another ship was hit by a suicide plane. It was over the horizon but looked like a big fire.

Suddenly, a big ship was bearing down on us.

"I hope they see us," I thought.

A destroyer escort (DE) looks very big if you are in the water looking up at it. They saw us. They were stopping. There was a lot of yelling on deck and they threw a cargo net over the side. Two sailors were ordered over the side to help us.

Someone at the rail yelled, "Save the officer first." They had seen my hat.

The sailor who "saved" me almost drowned me. I swallowed more salt water in the last six feet than I had in the whole night. Meanwhile, no one was helping my wounded sailor.

In a very sloppy manner, we all made it aboard. When I told the captain of the DE who I was, he seemed in doubt. It seems that as they picked up survivors of the LSM 59, the ships called in to the admiral's staff about any known casualties. Some sailor reported that he saw the captain go down with the ship.

"The ship turned over on top of him," he said. This message had made the rounds of the radio shacks at Okinawa. It was never corrected and my folks got letters from officers who had known me and got the bad word that night. Fortunately, my folks heard from me before they got those letters.

They would have started Rogers and me home the next day by air, but I was afraid that with us gone the crew might end up unloading ships while they waited for a ride home. I insisted they send us all together and they did.

It was a great big transport ship that had been a luxury liner before the war. I slept with other officers in a large open room with bunks two high. The crew was about four decks down. I played bridge most of the time and loved it. Everybody made their own bed but me. The officers around me wondered about it. One morning when I came back from breakfast I caught Joe Duckett making my bed and putting my clothes away.

"How are you getting along, Joe?"

"Just fine, Captain. Just fine."

"Does the crew need me for anything?"

"No, sir. We have nothing to do but play cards and shoot the breeze."

June 28, 1945

Dear Mother and Dad,

Everything is going well. I am healthy, happy, and looking toward the future with interest. I know that these letters are causing a lot of curiosity on your part, but as long as you don't worry, that is all that matters. If there were anything wrong with me, I would tell you in a hurry, as no one likes sympathy more than I, but having been born under a lucky star that never goes behind a cloud, you can rest assured that the "bad penny" will always turn up again.

I am awaiting orders to go to another theatre, and I may have difficulty in writing while I am en route. I don't know what theatre it will be, but I have hopes that it will be the Waldo Movie Theatre, in Kansas City.

By the way, I finished Chapter Two of Volume Two of the saga. I expect to get Volume Two finished very shortly.

Love, Dave

July 2, 1945

Dear Mother and Dad,

With luck, I may be home by the end of August. I would rather be there in the fall than in the summer. It has been summer ever since I joined the Navy, and I would like to go home and see the leaves turn red. Maybe George and I can get together after he graduates from Midshipman's School.

It is a very soft life that I am leading now. In fact, this whole tour of duty on the "59" has been a very soft one. I was sorry to leave the "59", as it was a good home, but my shoulders can stand a little rest from the responsibility. You can rest assured that my exit was a creditable one to the name of Hawley.

Love, Dave

CHAPTER 5
CIVILIAN LIFE

Survivor's Bureau, Washington DC

After I called my folks from San Francisco, I proceeded directly to Washington, D.C. My orders were to report to the Survivors Bureau, which I did. An attractive Wave yeoman first class assigned me a desk and told me to report for work the next morning at eight o'clock. She said, "Don't stay up too late. You have a lot of work to do."

I then went to Major Lamb's house and received a warm welcome from my cousin Betty. She and Harold insisted that I stay with them as I knew they would. I also called an old friend, Maxine Hattaway, and we went out.

The next day, I reported to the Survivors Bureau at nine o'clock and got a good bawling out from the pretty Wave. She gave me a list of things that I had to do. It included being interviewed by every department of the Navy. They want to know, among other things, if we had the right equipment and if we had the right training. Did we do everything we could have done to hold down the loss of lives and to keep the ship from sinking? My job also included answering the first two letters that came back from the next of kin from the men who were killed. When I complained about how long the list was, the pretty Wave smiled and said, "Tomorrow, Lt. Ed Rogers will arrive to help you." That pleased me.

One day after I had been there about a week, I got a note to call an Admiral Kimberly. When I got him on the phone, he said, "Do you know who I am?"

I replied, "No, sir. I am afraid I don't."

He said, "My son, George, was standing on the bridge of your ship when it was hit by the suicide plane." For a minute, I couldn't think who he was talking about. Then it dawned on me and I said, "You mean George, the gunnery officer from the admiral's staff?"

"That's right. George has told us all about you, and my wife and I are anxious to meet you. I am wondering if you could come out to our house for dinner some night this week."

I spent a very nice evening having dinner with the Admiral and his wife. George had really made a hero out of me. His father said the crew was so well trained in evacuating the ship, they acted like they had been waiting for this to happen.

George's older brother was the captain of a new destroyer that was being outfitted in Boston. If I wanted the job, the Admiral would call his son and see if he had been assigned an executive officer or if the job was still open. I said, "Yes. I would love to be the exec on a new destroyer." The Admiral said he would keep me posted.

In some of my interviews, I spent the time answering questions. These were not so bad. What I didn't like was when some interviewing officer would say, "Tell us your story." I didn't know where my story started. I was getting tired of telling it, and I was getting to where I wasn't sure I believed it. I told Rogers, "The next time someone asks me, 'How did you lose your ship?' I am going to say the exec officer ran it aground."

The next day I had an appointment to be interviewed by the ordinance department and they invited me to stand behind a podium in a room that was built like a small auditorium or classroom. There were about six officers in the seats and one of them said, "Tell us your story."

I said, "I don't know what story you want me to tell. I assume since this is the ordinance department, you want to know what experience was with the guns on the LSM."

They asked if we fired at the plane that hit our ship. They asked about past experiences and the use of our guns. When they heard I had been at Iwo Jima and the Solomons, they decided the Admiral should be hearing my story. We took a recess.

When we reassembled after the coffee break, my audience had grown from half a dozen officers to maybe fifteen. The officer who had called the break took over. "Gentlemen, to bring you up to date, Lieutenant Hawley was the captain of an LSM at Okinawa that was sunk by a suicide plane. He has just told us that not only did his guns fail to fire at the suicide plane at Okinawa, he landed on Iwo Jima on D-Day and ordered his gun crews to lie down in the gun tubs because it was his experience that the exposure that gun crews faced on a landing ship was too great for any damage they inflicted on the enemy because they couldn't see the enemy and didn't know where the targets were. Do I have that right, Lieutenant?"

"Yes, sir."

"All right. I suggest we have the Lieutenant review for us the experience he has had that brought him to this conclusion."

I started in and told them the whole story of how we were ordered to take the *Barry* out and get it sunk. Then I told them of the landings I had made with the LCT324. The questions went on till six o'clock. I was so tired when I got to Betty and Harold's house for supper, I almost didn't go over to Maxine's that night.

Saturday Evening Post

The next day, I got a call from a Robert Yoder who said he was an associate editor of the *Saturday Evening Post*. He had been part of my audience the day before and they would like for me to come to Philadelphia to the Curtis Publishing Company where they could write an article about my war experiences. He had made a deal with the Navy's public relations department and the Navy was willing to let me go. Did I want to do it? Yes, I said. I would like to take a break from what I was doing. He said they would pay all my expenses and if they couldn't pay me money, they would try to figure out something nice to do for me.

They showed me a very good time. At the end of the week, they said they had all the material they needed and they would like to pay my expenses on a trip somewhere. Where did I want to go? I thought it over and said New York City. When I was back there as a midshipman, I had no money. I would like to go back there and see the town in style.

My brother, George, was in Midshipman's School in New York and I wrote his commanding officer and asked if he could have a couple days off to entertain his hero brother. I also asked Maxine if she would like to go to New York. I don't know what she told the Navy, but she showed up about the same time George did. The three of us had a marvelous time.

We went to the most expensive places we could think of on the *Saturday Evening Post.* When the time was up, Maxine and I went back to Washington.

Thorne & Lake Leelaneau

Unbeknownst to me, while we were gone, my cousin Betty had written a letter to Thorne Gray in Monroe, Michigan. She had said that if Thorne had any idea of marrying Dave Hawley she better take some affirmative action. She told Thorne I was going over to see Maxine every night. I don't know whether Betty knew that Maxine was in New York.

The night that Harry Truman said the war with Japan was over was a big night for me. The next morning I went down and told the Admiral I didn't want to be on his son's new destroyer.

When I got the thirty-day leave I had been promised for two years, I had a letter in my pocket from Thorne Gray inviting me to come to Lake Leelaneau. I decided I would go there before I went home. It was August and that is when you go there.

When I got off the plane at Traverse City, Michigan, I called my Uncle Bill at Lake Leelaneau to come and pick me up. Lake Leelaneau is twenty miles outside Traverse City. I had spent several happy summer vacations there as a guest of Uncle Bill and Aunt Eva. They didn't have any boys of their own and they treated me like I was their own son. Their cottage was about a quarter of a mile down the beach from the Grays' cottage.

Although I had never had any romance with Thorne, she was always in the group that I played with. We swam, sailed, canoed, rode an aqua plane behind a fast boat, played tennis, and went to the movies in a group. JS Gray and his wife, Kippie, Thorne's parents, were my Uncle Bill and Aunt Eva's best friends. They were neighbors at the Lake and they were also neighbors at home in Monroe, Michigan. We had eaten many meals at their house and they had eaten many meals at our house. When I had asked Thorne to come to Houston to help me have a good time, I think her folks were not sure it was a good idea, but they didn't try to stop her. Her father had always liked me.

Uncle Bill picked me up at the plane and drove me to their cottage where I had spent many happy days. Aunt Eva was thrilled to see me and we had a wonderful visit. In the middle of the afternoon, I walked down to the Grays' house. Thorne was there alone. Her folks had gone on a fishing trip and were due back that night.

When I left Washington, D.C., I had halfway made up my mind that I was going to marry Maxine Hattaway. She was no beauty, but she was smart, had a good sense of humor, and was a real nice person. Furthermore, she was crazy about me. Thorne and I began comparing notes and I found she had halfway made up her mind to marry a Navy officer that was a friend of her brother's. Her brother had brought Todd home on a visit and he had fallen for Thorne. I told Thorne about Maxine. We talked about how much fun we had had in Houston and I asked Thorne why she never wrote to me. She said the deal was when I invited her to Houston that there would be no strings attached. When the visit was over, it was over .

After a while, I said to her, "Are you in love with this Todd that you are thinking about marrying?" She thought a minute and said, "No. I guess I'm not."

"Then why do you want to marry him?"

She thought for a minute and said, "I think the reason is that I feel he really needs me." I began to laugh. She looked shocked and angry.

I said, "Thorne, if he really needs you he must be a weak sister. You couldn't hold up a paper bag. You start crying whenever things don't go just right. You need to marry somebody strong like me that can hold you up."

Thorne was furious. She began pounding on me and calling me names. I got up and left and went back to Uncle Bill's house.

I told Uncle Bill I wanted to catch the first plane in the morning for Kansas City and he agreed to drive me in. He insisted we stop at Grays' so I could say hello and goodbye to JS and Kippie. I gave Thorne a big kiss and hug to satisfy her mother and father. Then, I flew home to Kansas City.

Goodbye Maxine, Hello Thorne

My folks were overjoyed to see me. They showed me off to all their friends and neighbors. My exploits were written up in the *Kansas City Star* and I was the speaker at my dad's War Dad chapter.

After I had been home about two weeks, my mother gave a dinner party for me. The guests were all of my parents generation. I had written a short note to Thorne apologizing for being mean to her and asking her to forgive me. I had received an answer back that surprised me. It said, "I have been thinking it over, and I think you are probably right. I should marry somebody like you. Somebody who is familiar with my weaknesses and won't be disappointed. So, if you really meant what you said, I guess that I would be willing to marry you."

I couldn't think exactly what I had said that brought this on. I had the letter in my pocket when I went to my mother's dinner party.

One of my mother's bridge playing friends, said, for all to hear, "Does David have a girlfriend?" My mother smiled and said, "I don't believe so. He just hasn't come to that point in his life yet."

I thought, I'm twenty-six years old. If I am not interested in girls, I must be pretty slow in maturing. There was a telephone on a stand in a corner of the dining room. It had a long cord and I got up and set it on the table in front of me. In front of the assembled guests, I called Western Union and said I wanted to send a telegram to Thorne Gray, RFD 3, Traverse City, Michigan. The message is, "Let's get married next Wednesday. Call me with the answer when you get this telegram. Love, Dave."

My mother and father looked stunned and the rest of the guests applauded. My mother quickly recovered herself and told the guests that she had known Thorne since Thorne was a girl and always liked her. She said Thorne came from a fine family and her father was the publisher of the newspaper in the town where my mother grew up.

After the guests had left, I called Edward H. Rogers, Jr. in West Hampton Beach, New York. I told him I had just sent a telegram to Thorne Gray asking her to marry me next Wednesday and I wanted him to be the best man. He said, "What makes you think she will say yes?" I said, "She came to Houston, didn't she?"

September 11, 1945, Thorne wrote me back, "Davey, I love you. I want nothing more in this world than to marry you and spend my life with you. Feeling this and admitting it to myself has made me happier than I ever thought I could be. Everything seems brighter, even the sun."

I sent back a telegram: "I would like to marry you as soon as possible. Let's get married next week. Call me tomorrow morning."

I had already accepted an invitation from my sister and her husband to go on a roller skating party on Tuesday night. They had fixed me up with a date with the older sister of a girl that my brother George had been going with. Against my parents loud protests, I went ahead and kept the date. We had a marvelous time and when I took her home, she made quite a speech.

My date said, "I had a marvelous time tonight. I don't know where you have been. My sister has been going with your brother and we all admire him, but I never heard of you. Now that we have found this good thing, I think we should continue it. The young people in our church are having a picnic Sunday and I wonder if you would like to go?"

I said, "I, too, had a marvelous time tonight. But I won't be able to go Sunday. I am leaving tomorrow to get married." That was thc cnd of that romance.

When Thorne's father got the word, he was attending a meeting in Washington, D.C. He called me and said, "I am thrilled that you and Thorne have decided to get married. Nothing could please me more. However, there is no reason to rush into it. I think you should wait until you get out of the Navy and Thorne finishes her course at Northwestern. Then, when you know what you are going to do for a living and where you are going to live, we can plan the wedding."

I said, "JS, with all due respect, Thorne and I are going to get married next Wednesday. I certainly hope that you will be there to give the bride away. But, if you're not, we are going to get married anyway."

He said, "We'll see about that." And hung up. About an hour later, he called back and said, "Congratulations. I'll be there."

We got married September 19, 1945. JS was not only there, he had completely decorated that house for the wedding. Thorne and her mother were members of the Christian Science Church and her father either didn't go at all or he visited with them. The Christian Science Church does not have weddings or funerals in the church. Therefore, we were married in Thorne's home. It was a beautiful home with a beautiful staircase for Thorne and her father to come down. Ed Rogers was there as my best man and all of my relatives except my brother George. The Navy wouldn't let him off.

JS and I had discussed how Thorne and I were to leave town after the reception. I had three more days of leave and then I reported to the Great Lakes Naval Base outside of Chicago. JS suggested we spend our wedding night at the Commodore Perry Hotel in Toledo. We could borrow his Buick to get there and leave it in the hotel's garage for him to pick up the next day.

When we arrived at the Commodore Perry, I told the doorman to put the car in their garage and JS Gray would be coming for it. Thorne sat down on a settee in the lobby surrounded by rice and our pile of luggage. I got in the line at the front desk. It was a big lobby and every chair in it was occupied. There were a few people standing and there were four or five people in the line at the front desk. When my turn came and I gave the clerk my name, he looked through a big file on the counter and turned to me and said, "Lieutenant, I am terribly sorry, but we can't take care of you." I said, "I have a reservation, and a telegram confirming it." And with that I handed him the telegram. He looked at it and said, "This is correct, but you didn't tell us that you would arrive late. At ten o'clock we sell all the reservations that haven't notified us that they would arrive late." I said, "Look. I got married tonight. I have to have a room. If you don't have a room in this hotel, find me a room in some other hotel."

I returned to where Thorne was sitting surrounded by our luggage. "We're in big trouble. I didn't tell the hotel that we were going to get here late and they sold the reservation at ten o'clock. The hotel is full. In fact, he says the whole town is full and we should drive on to whatever direction we are going."

"If the room clerk won't talk to you, ask to see the manager," she said. " Go see him and tell him we have no car to go anywhere else in."

I went back and told Thorne, "He was a really nice fellow, but he couldn't help us. "

She said, "You sit down and watch the bags."

Thorne was gone less than ten minutes. When she returned, she sat down and said, "Go over to the desk clerk and get our key."

CHAPTER 6
FAMILY MAN

Married Life

Thorne was accustomed to standing up for what she thought was right. After she graduated from high school, she went one year to Mount Vernon, a girls preparatory school in Washington, D.C. Then she went three years to Vassar. Among her activities at Vassar, she rode with a busload to Washington, D.C. to protest the passage of the draft law. While they were in Washington, D.C. they would not eat in any restaurant that did not serve Blacks. Those restaurants were hard to find in 1940. She majored in music at Vassar and by the end of her third year, she had decided she had no talent to create music and would never be good enough to be a professional performer. So, she did not return her Senior year but went to work for the newspaper her father ran.

After three years on the newspaper, she quit to go to Journalism school at Northwestern University in Evanston, Illinois. She was twenty-five years old and a student at Northwestern when we were married. She was living in a one-room efficiency apartment in Evanston and I moved in with her.

I was attending a three-week training school at the Great Lakes Naval Training Center. The school amounted to nothing compared to my other jobs in the Navy and after a week of it, I woke up one morning not feeling well and decided I wouldn't go that day. I would stay home and let my new wife nurse me. My mother had never been very sympathetic to me except when I was sick. When I said I didn't feel well, she would flutter all over me. I expected the same or more so from Thorne. That morning, after the Navy had been warned not to expect me, I lay back in bed while Thorne fixed a little breakfast. I thought, "the nursing comes next." After she did the breakfast dishes, she started cleaning the apartment. I kept wondering, "When does the sympathy start?" She cleaned the bathroom and the kitchen. She organized her clothes. When she finally finished, it was time to fix lunch. After she did the lunch dishes, I thought the quiet sympathy time had finally arrived. She stepped into the clothes closet and when she came out she had her hat on.

I said, "Where are you going?"

She said, "I am going to a movie. I will give you a chance to sleep."

I was so astonished, I never said a word. I had never been to a movie by myself in my whole life and I hadn't been to a movie in the afternoon since I cut school in high school. I lay there all afternoon while Thorne was gone, wondering what action I should take, if any. When she returned and hung up her hat, I said, "How was the movie?"

She said, "Oh, it was a good movie, but I had seen it before."

That really shocked me. She would rather see a movie she had seen before, than spend the afternoon with me.

Each afternoon, when my school was out, I took the train into Evanston where I transferred to the "elevated." At the station one day, I met a sailor who had been on another LSM who recognized me. I was so glad to see someone who had been in the same war I was in, I insisted on buying him a beer. We had several beers and when our party broke up, I realized I was going to be late for dinner. I passed a floral shop on my way home and I went in. I told the clerk I had been married thirteen days and this was the first time I had been late for dinner. He said, "Buy thirteen roses. That will get her."

When I walked in the door with the roses, Thorne said, "Don't take your hat off. We're going out to dinner as soon as I put these roses in water."

I said, "I'm kinda tired. I'd just as soon stay home tonight."

"No. I have already thrown the dinner out. We're going out and kick up our heels. I want you to remember the next time you feel like going out and having some fun, to come home and get me." We went out and saw the night life in Evanston, and I got the message. She didn't want to sit at home with the dinner cooked and wait for me to get ready to come home. If I wanted to go out and have some fun and do a little socializing, I was to come and get her first. There is nothing like starting a marriage out right.

After three weeks at the Great Lakes Training Center, they sent me to the Navy Base outside of Memphis, Tennessee. Thorne and I got a room at the Chase Hotel in Memphis and I took the bus out to the base. On the third day when I came home, Thorne said that she had done some exploring and had rented us a room with kitchen privileges in the little town of Millington, which was right next the Navy base.

Thorne got a civil service job on the Navy base, but there was nothing to do in Millington in the evenings and it was too big a deal to take a bus into Memphis, so Thorne and I spent the evenings walking on the country roads heading out of the town. In the quiet of those evening walks, we quietly fell in love.

One night, after partying with friends, I woke up and couldn't breathe. I tried to tell Thorne what was wrong with me, but all I could do was rattle. I was still trying to tell her when the ambulance from the Naval Hospital arrived. Mrs. Goldsby, our landlady, had heard me and called the ambulance. I was very sick the next day. The doctor told Thorne I had pneumonia.

A week later, I was a little better, but not much. Thorne went to the commandant of the hospital and said I wanted out of the hospital and out of the Navy. He said, no, Lieutenant Hawley was not well enough to release. At the end of four more days, I felt I was about the same, but Thorne said I was getting worse. She went back to the commandant. "The war is over. He has done his part. Let me take him home." The answer was still, "No." She finally wore him down.

"Get A Job!"

We went to Monroe, Michigan and Thorne's home. We moved into Thorne's old room where she had grown up. In thirty days I was completely well. It was the first of December, 1945. We had been at Thorne's house for a month. That night, Thorne had gone up to bed and her dad, JS, and I were alone in the living room. He put down his paper and said, "Dave, I have been thinking about what you are going to do for a living. You have three choices, as I see it. The first is that you can go to work for me on my paper. The second is you go to work for one of my friends on their paper. And the third is, you can go to journalism school and learn something about the newspaper business so you can be of some value to the paper you work for. I think you ought to talk it over with Thorne and decide which it is going to be. The sooner you decide, the sooner we can get on with it."

Between gambling and investing in the stock market, I had accumulated some cash. Consequently, when I was released to inactive duty, I had eight thousand dollars in the bank. I felt rich and I was not in a hurry to get a job and go to work.

When I went upstairs, Thorne was still awake. I told her what her father had said. She said, "What do you want to do?"

"Let's go to Kansas City tomorrow and stay with my folks for a while."

When we told JS in the morning that we had decided to go to Kansas City he seemed perfectly happy. He even volunteered to give us a car to go in. It was a 1936 Ford.

My father was not as patient as JS had been. When we had been there one week, he came home from work and found me with my new wife sitting on the davenport and drinking a beer. He said, "When are you going to start looking for a job?"

I told him I wasn't in a hurry to get a job. I told him about my eight thousand dollars and said I thought I would spend a few months getting my health back. He was not sympathetic with this plan. He said, "Dave, you can't work for me and you can't live here. No house is big enough for two women."

I didn't start looking for a job, but he kept pushing. I had been wondering if I would like to write a book, and I got my typewriter out and spent a couple hours a day at the dining room table. About three days later, my dad came home and announced that he had found the place where I should work.

Working for Henry Ford

My dad said I should go out to the Ford Motor Company the next morning and apply for a job as a Henry Ford Trainee. I resisted. After three days of resisting, I finally broke down and went out to the Ford plant just to prove he was wrong.

I felt sure I couldn't get a job as a Henry Ford Trainee through the Ford employment office, so I didn't even stop there: I went directly to the Sales Office and got an interview. The Sales Manager asked, "What are you doing now?"

"Well, I am still on terminal leave from the Navy. While they are still paying me, I am writing a book."

"If you are writing a book, you must be a person who reads a lot."

We talked about authors, and my favorite, Thomas Wolfe. The Sales Manager was impressed. He took me to lunch, and later he got me an interview with the man in charge of the Trainee program. I was advised to make my speech and not let the man get a word in edgewise.

My speech began with how I had read the article in *Fortune* magazine and decided that the Ford Motor Company was where I wanted to make my career. I had almost finished talking when I paused for breath. When I did, he jumped up and grabbed my hand. "You're hired. You can start work tomorrow morning. I don't think you are half as smart as you say you are, but it will only cost us a couple months salary to find out. I'd be a damn fool not to find out."

When my father heard the news, he was really thrilled. When Thorne heard the news, she asked how much they were going to pay me. I confessed that I didn't know. It had never been brought up. She said, "Well, I'm sure the Ford Motor Company can afford to pay you what you are worth."

Suits were hard to find in December of 1945, but I bought an ugly brown pinstripe at the Richman Clothing Company in Kansas City. After giving up on renting an apartment, I bought a house on Lake Lotawana for sixty-five hundred dollars cash. It had originally been a summer cottage, but the last owner had put a large furnace in it and converted it into a year-round house. There was no insulation in the house whatsoever and when the cold winds blew, they would go right through the house.

I reported for work Monday morning, was assigned a desk, and introduced around the office. I was also introduced to the time clock and told to punch it when I arrived in the morning. Lake Lotawana and the Ford Plant were both on the east side of Kansas City so it was almost all highway driving. It took thirty minutes to drive it. The first three days I was late to work every morning. My boss decided I didn't need to punch the time clock, but should do my best to get to work on time.

It turned out they didn't have an organized training program like the one in *Fortune* magazine. I spent a few weeks learning what the department heads did, spent time in the labor relations office, and learned how to read financial statements.

The Ford dealers had not had any cars in four years and many dealers had gone out of business. They had started to make cars again and they needed the dealer's organization operating. I started calling on Ford dealers in northwestern Kansas, to Great Bend, Russell or Hays. After I had called on all the dealers in northwestern Kansas, they changed my zone to southern Missouri. New cars were at a premium. Every dealer had lists of customers waiting for a new car. I was the zone manager who controlled the number of new cars the dealer received. I was beginning to feel confident and enjoy my job but I was learning there was more to it than acting smart and going to the small town Rotary Clubs for lunch.

Medals of Honor

One day I got a letter from the United States Navy saying that I was to appear at the United States Air Station at Olathe, Kansas on a certain day at a certain time, with my dress uniform on to receive the Silver Star medal for gallantry in action. At the bottom of the letter, there was a line that said, if for any reason, it is impossible for me to attend at this time please notify them at such and such telephone number. I called the number and told the lady that answered that I would be unable to attend. She said, "Then we will change the date." I said, "No. I can't come at all. You just mail the medal to me." So, instead of receiving the Silver Star from the admiral while the troops stood at attention and the band played "The Conquering Hero," I got my Silver Star in the mail. It was probably unfair to my parents and my wife.

About a month later, I received a similar letter saying I should appear to receive a Bronze Star medal. I called them up and said if I wouldn't come out there to get a Silver Star, I surely wouldn't come out to get a Bronze Star. So they mailed that also. The citation that came with the Silver Star medal was on the stationery of the Secretary of the Navy and said:

"The President of the United States takes pleasure in presenting the SILVER STAR MEDAL to LIEUTENANT DAVID CHARLES HAWLEY United States Naval Reserve for service as set forth in the following CITATION:

"For conspicuous gallantry and intrepidity as commanding officer of the U.S.S. LSM 59 in action against enemy Japanese forces during the assault on Okinawa on June 21, 1945. Immediately organizing a fire-fighting party when an enemy suicide plane crashed on board and set fire to his ship, Lieutenant Hawley personally manned a fire extinguisher and, with his ship rapidly sinking, jumped to a narrow ledge near the blaze to aid in fighting the fire. By his courage and determination in the face of grave hazards, Lieutenant Hawley inspired several of his crew to close in and fight the fire more vigorously, thereby preventing greater loss of life and injury to personnel. His leadership throughout was in keeping with the highest traditions of the United States Naval Service.

For the President,
John L. Sullivan
Secretary of the Navy

The citation that came with my Bronze Star medal arrived about a month later. It also was on the stationery of the Secretary of the Navy, and it said the following:

"The President of the United States takes pleasure in presenting the BRONZE STAR MEDAL to LIEUTENANT DAVID CHARLES HAWLEY United States Naval Reserve for service as set forth in the following CITATION:

"For meritorious service as officer-in-charge of LCT 324 during the assault and occupation of the Japanese held New Georgia, Treasury and Bougainville Islands of the Solomon Group, from June 30, 1943 to March 16, 1944. Working tirelessly and often under enemy fire, Lieutenant (then Lieutenant Junior Grade) Hawley rendered invaluable service in providing a continuous flow of vitally needed supplies to our troops during the fighting for these strategic islands. By his expert seamanship, sound judgment and devotion to duty, Lieutenant Hawley contributed materially to the success of the Solomon Islands campaign and upheld the highest traditions of the United States Naval Service.

Lieutenant Hawley is authorized to wear the Combat "V."

For the President,
James Forrestal
Secretary of the Navy

My mother had my citations framed, including the one for the Navy Marine Corps Medal which Halsey had given me in the Pacific. It had to be the gunnery officer from the admiral's staff that was standing on the bridge when the ship was hit, that had recommended me for the medal.

Challenges

Meanwhile, life went on at Lake Lotawana. I would leave town on Monday morning and head for western Kansas or southern Missouri and not come back until Friday night. Thorne and our dog, Max, were there alone. That winter the snow piled up and closed the road. No one plowed it. The wind would blow through that house like it was a screened-in porch. The summer cottages around us were boarded up till spring.

We had made some wonderful new friends at the Lake, but they lived quite a distance from us. Our closest year-round neighbors were Betty and Oz Feazel. Oz Feazel was a TWA captain; his wife, Betty, was a Wellesley graduate. When we knew we were going to spend the evening with them, we would pick a subject and read up on it, then discuss it. Although we disagreed with many of their thoughts and ideas, we found them very stimulating. They were warm, intelligent people who were interested in discussing any subject we brought up.

When we went over there in the evening, Betty always wore a long skirt that brushed the floor, and she was barefoot. They had a large attractive living room with a Steinway grand piano in one corner. Thorne had taken piano lessons all her life and she majored in music at Vassar. She loved the Feazel's piano. Now, she and Betty could have piano recitals. It gave Thorne something to do while I was out of town.

When I drove in on Friday night, I had spent the last four or five hours driving that car as fast as it would run. I was wound up like a dollar watch and it took me all Friday night to relax. Sometimes, I drank too much in the process, and felt bad on Saturday. Thorne and I were in love-land and we made love on the weekends. Whoever it was that said that sex was the most overrated thing in the world, was undoubtedly not twenty-six years old. The sleeping porch on that house was all glass. It was on the side of a steep hill and the tops of the trees were outside our windows. It was like making love in a tree house. I loved it. It wasn't long before Thorne was pregnant.

In November of 1946, we had lived at the Lake almost a year. I had worked at the Ford Motor Company for almost a year. We had been married fourteen months and Thorne's baby was due. Her mother, Kippie, came to help. After ten days of waiting for the baby with no results, Thorne woke me in the middle of the night and said, "Get up. This is it."

It was a cold night with a very light snow. I had called the hospital and the doctor and they met us at the door. After Thorne reached the labor room, the pains stopped. Kippie and I sat down in the waiting room to wait. The waiting room was cold and drafty. I had a bad cold and felt miserable. My folks lived less than ten minutes away. Without explanation I left the hospital and drove to my folks' house to get some rest. The next morning, my mother woke me and said Kippie was on the phone. Kippie said, "Thorne is in the delivery room now, and if you hurry down here, she may never find out where you spent the night." I got there in time to greet the doctor when he came out of the delivery room. He said, "You have a son who appears to have the right number of everything." I said, "How is my wife?" He said, "Any woman who can have babies that easily ought to have a dozen." I don't think Kippie ever forgave me for not waiting in the waiting room while Roger was born.

New cars were very difficult to buy as every dealer had long lists of orders. I was one of the few people who could buy one. I bought a new yellow Ford convertible and we both loved it. It gave me a lift every time I got in it. I felt proud when I saw Thorne driving it with Roger sitting in the car seat beside her. Everybody should have a convertible when they are young.

Our life at the Lake was very pleasant on the whole. Our biggest problem was that Roger threw up whenever we picked him up. Our clothes all smelled of spit-up. The whole house smelled of spit-up. In addition to being unpleasant, Roger wasn't gaining any weight. From the time he was six months old until he was a year and a half old, he never gained an ounce.

Thorne was taking Roger to a doctor on the Plaza twice a week to try to cure his spit-ups. We were very worried about him.

My sister Harriett and her husband George Clay had a two-year-old girl, Connie, and a four-year-old boy, Cotton, who had something wrong with him. The doctors weren't sure what was wrong with him, but he had developed severe bronchitis and wasn't making any progress in throwing it off. The doctor finally recommended that Harriett take Cotton to Arizona to see if the climate would help him, so they rented a house on a dude ranch just outside of Tucson. George Clay worked for TWA in Kansas City and he flew down to Tucson every Friday and spent the weekend with his family. During the week he lived alone in their three-bedroom house in Kansas City.

Their house was in a good neighborhood close to my folks' house and not far from our doctor. We rented our house at Lotawana and moved in with George Clay. I was always gone during the week; George, Thorne and Roger would share the house during the week. Weekends George went to Tucson; while he was catching his plane, I would arrive with my suitcase at the house. For the first six weeks we lived there, I never saw George Clay.

One Friday night, I met George and Thorne for dinner and we sat with some old friends of George Clay's. Conversation was lively with the three of us doing a lot of catching up. The other woman at the table asked Thorne, "Which of these men do you belong to?"

Thorne said, pointing to me, "I live with him from Friday night until he leaves town on Monday morning. Then, George comes in on Monday night and stays until Friday morning."

Still looking at the woman, Thorne said, "Does your husband travel?"

"Yes, my husband travels a great deal, and I don't have anybody that fills in when he is gone."

"That's too bad. You ought to work on that." We had never thought how our arrangement must look to the neighbors until we had this conversation. The next day, George called the neighbors.

We lived in the Clays' house the winter of '47 and the spring of '48. We saw a lot of my folks, it was handy to the doctor's office, it was warm, and George Clay was a peach. I think Thorne learned more housekeeping that winter from George than she ever learned from her mother. He never went to bed without picking up the downstairs and emptying the ash trays.

In the spring of 1948, I figured with the advent of warm weather Harriett would be coming home. I started looking for a house to buy.

I met a man who had just learned that he was being transferred to Oklahoma. His house was just what we needed. It was a big old ugly house at 611 West 59th Terrace. That was close to my folks' house and not far from the Clays'. If I could come up with two thousand dollars, I could buy it that afternoon before he gave it to a real estate agent. I didn't have the money, but I knew where I could get it.

Thorne was playing bridge with some ladies. I didn't want to explain the whole deal to Thorne and the ladies. I took my set of keys and went and got the yellow convertible which was parked in front of the house where she was. I drove it down to Rudy Fick's used car lot and sold it for twenty-two hundred dollars. It was a '47 which I had bought new at dealer's cost for fourteen hundred dollars. When Thorne found her car was gone, her hostess wanted her to call the police, but Thorne called me. I told her we had bought a new house.

Thorne was pregnant when we moved into our new house and the neighbors all cheered when she went to the hospital in September of 1948 to give birth to Harriett, our second child. Thorne's mother, Kippie, came to help and she and I went dancing every night of Thorne's hospital stay. We also had a baby nurse, Mrs. Parker, to take care of the baby the first two weeks. Everything went well. Roger stopped spitting up shortly before Harriett was born. He started gaining weight and looking normal. The Ford Motor Company kept giving me raises and continuing my education.

I had attended the Wornall Road Baptist Church from the time I was a small boy until I went to war. I went to Sunday School until I was old enough to go to church with my parents and not squirm and whisper. When I was eleven, I joined the church and was baptized. My mother was an active Circle member and we almost always attended the Wednesday night dinners. Church meant a lot to my mother. I was in the Boy Scout troop that met in the church basement. My sister was married in that church. When we lived at Lotawana, it was too far to come to church in Kansas City, but now that we were back in the old neighborhood, I renewed my membership in the Wornall Road Baptist Church. They welcomed me back like the Prodigal Son and we were very happy there.

The Young Father, Absentee Wife

It was September of 1949. I had been married four years, and I was thirty years old. We had a boy, Roger, who was three, and a girl, Harriett, who was one and a half. We lived in a seven room house with a large FHA mortgage in a nice neighborhood. I had a good job traveling for the Ford Motor Company. Sometimes they called us district sales representatives and sometimes they called us zone managers, but I called on thirty-two Ford dealers in central Kansas and sold them their new cars and told them how Mr. Ford wanted them to operate their business. I worked harder and made more money than most of my contemporaries. I was gone from home from Monday morning until Friday night every week. The weekends I spent with my wife and the two kids. Sometimes we played tennis at Loose Park with my sister and her husband. But mostly, I worked around the house and played with the kids. We were very happy.

My boss, everybody's boss, Paul Larsen, had been transferred, promoted to Detroit. On a Friday night the office had a going-away party for him at the Muehlebach Hotel downtown. It was a cocktail party with office personnel, the department heads, the road men like me, and a few of Mr. Larsen's favorite dealers. The party lasted into the wee hours with lots of drinking and story-telling.

When I got home at four a.m. I was surprised to find Thorne waiting up for me. She said she didn't feel well and she was more comfortable sitting up. I thought she was making excuses for worrying about me and hurried us both into bed. Early the next morning, Thorne woke me up and said, "Do something about Harriett. She is awake and wanting to get up and I don't feel like it." I didn't feel like it, either, but since she so seldom asked me to get up with the kids, I felt there must be big trouble. I got up and took care of Harriett and Roger with Thorne's instructions, but I felt terrible. Thorne got up around noon and said she guessed she was all right. I thought she was just worn out with the kids. We went to bed early that night, and Thorne still didn't feel like doing anything on Sunday. I had to leave town the next day and we had two little kids to take care of. Against Thorne's better judgment, I called Dr. Meyers Sunday afternoon. Dr. Meyers was my father's age and had been our family doctor for years. Thorne thought he was an alarmist. He examined Thorne Sunday afternoon and couldn't find anything wrong with her. Thorne told him how she had just come back from a very active vacation in Michigan where, among other things, she had taken a twenty-mile hike. She had been playing a lot of tennis, taking care of two babies, and she was worn out. Dr. Meyers said the only way he could give Thorne a thorough examination, which she should have, was for her to come in and spend half a day at St. Mary's Hospital. He pushed it. I pushed it and Thorne finally agreed.

After the tests were run, Dr. Meyers took me in a small office to talk to me. "Dave, I am sorry to have to tell you this. Thorne has tuberculosis. I was afraid she did when I talked to her yesterday. Dr. Mantz is the best specialist in Kansas City. He has looked at the x-rays, examined her and say there is no doubt.

"She will have to go to a sanitarium and have complete bed rest. The best thing would be if we could get her into Leeds Sanitarium. It is close, and you could visit her."

"How soon will she have to go?"

"Today if we can get her in. She should go in an ambulance. Why don't you go and tell her while I see if we can get her in?"

I went in and told Thorne. Naturally, she wanted to know who was going to take care of Roger and Harriett. How long was she going to be there? While I was still telling her that I didn't know, the ambulance driver was at the door. Thorne said, "This is ridiculous. I walked in here this morning feeling fine and now they are taking me away in an ambulance."

I went to Leeds and was interviewed by the Business Manager. He asked me how much money I made, what did I own, and what I owed. What were my problems going to be operating a household without a wife? I asked him how long my wife was going to be there. He was a kind, sympathetic man, but he said he was a business man and not a doctor.

I couldn't go and see Thorne until visiting hours. I waited until three o'clock when the woman said the head doctor would be there. He came in about four o'clock and was obviously terribly hurried and harried. I asked him how long my wife would be there. He said he didn't know. I asked how long did people usually stay there, and he said from six months up to the rest of their lives. He said they hadn't examined Thorne yet and didn't know what kind of shape she was in. I said she couldn't be very sick. She played tennis two days ago. He said somebody thought she was pretty sick or they wouldn't have sent her there. I went home and found my mother was exhausted from taking care of Roger and Harriett.

Until I got the kids fed and into bed, I was too busy to think. I found I was better off when I didn't have time to think. My father came over and listened to me worry out loud. The main problem was that I didn't know anything about tuberculosis and neither did he.

I called Dr. Mantz at two a.m. and told him he had examined my wife this morning at St. Mary's and they had sent her over to Leeds. I told him I couldn't find out what to expect from anybody and I was about to lose my mind. I told him I had two small children and I traveled for a living and I needed to talk to somebody that knew something. He said, "Why don't you come on out to my house right now."

I said, "I'm on my way."

When I got there, Dr. Mantz had his bathrobe and slippers on and coffee was bubbling in the pot. We sat in his living room and drank coffee while he told me that my wife's attitude would have a great deal to do with her recovery. And, he said, "Her attitude will be dependent to a great extent on your attitude." He said no one could convince Thorne that I was doing a good job taking care of the kids. I had to convince Thorne that I had all kinds of faith in her recovery. He said, "A good place to start is on your knees." He said, "I know you and Thorne can make it. I will help you all I can. I will examine Thorne and report to you, but the big job is your faith and courage and how it affects Thorne." It was starting to get light when I left there and I felt a whole lot better.

I went the next afternoon for my first visitor's day. Thorne was in a room with three other women who had not only had been there a long time, they were all repeaters. Thorne explained that a "repeater" had been returned to civilian life, supposedly cured, only to find out after several months that they really weren't cured but must return. A terrible cloud of gloom surrounded her bed. I was glad I had talked to Dr. Mantz. I realized how important it was that I stay strong. I said everything to her I could think of. When the time was up, I went to the office and demanded that she be moved to more favorable surroundings.

On September 27, 1949 I wrote to Thorne:

"When I came back to my hotel room tonight, I found that through the open window a bird had entered my room. When I entered the room, the bird was trying desperately to get out. I opened the window as wide as it would go and tried to shoo the bird out. The bird battered itself by flying into the walls, the ceiling, the mirror, and the closed part of the window. I tried turning off the lights, leaving the bird alone. While I was sitting here quietly watching the little sparrow regain its breath, I thought to myself if I only knew what to say to that little bird to get it to relax and let me help it, I could lift it out easily through the window to freedom again without hurting it a bit. But birds just naturally aren't that way.

"I started thinking that if I knew what to say to that bird, I would know what to say to my wife. The bird finally blundered through the open window to freedom again, as you undoubtedly will do. But how much easier if you and the bird would relax and have confidence in me, and let me gently lift you through the open window before you batter your head against all the walls.

"I have always had to smooth your feathers and relax you. But if I can just get to you so that I can pet you and talk to you, you settle down and purr like a kitten."

Love, Dave

The next thing was to find somebody who would stay with my children so I could start traveling again. My mother obviously couldn't. We didn't know how long Thorne would be in the hospital. Worst of all, Thorne was pregnant again.

The doctor said Thorne would not survive the pregnancy and she should have an abortion, but it was difficult to have the pregnancy terminated legally. While waiting to hear if an abortion could or should be done, I had to go to Wichita for an important sales meeting with Ford dealers.

I went to Wichita and conducted the meeting. After I had finished the presentation and supervised the signing of the agreements by the dealers, after the smiles and the handshakes and the jokes, I went to the telephone in my room and called Kansas City. We had not yet heard a decision from the doctor.

As I drove back to Kansas City, I had four hours to think about the problem and I decided it wasn't up to Dr. Mantz or anybody in the medical profession to make this decision. It was my life, my wife, and my baby. When I arrived in Kansas City, I drove directly to see Thorne. The decision was ours to make. Thorne said, "In that case, the decision is all made. We will have the baby, and I feel a great deal better about the whole thing. In fact, I am real happy." She meant it, too. She was radiant. How stupid I had been to ever doubt it.

I went to see Dr. Keeler, who had delivered Harriett, our second child. I told him about our situation, that Thorne was pregnant in a TB sanitarium and would need special care. He agreed to oversee her pregnancy and help deliver the baby when it was due.

I got home and started working on finding someone to care for our children and be a housekeeper. My brother, George, put the ad in the weekly *Kansas City Star*. This paper had a tremendous circulation in the rural Midwest. We got a bushel basket full of letters. Some of them sent their pictures. Most of them were from women who had children of their own and no husband, or at least they couldn't find their husband. I had no idea there were that many men that had run off. One letter said, "I will take a chance on you. You couldn't be as bad as the guy I am living with now."

My mother, father, George and I spent one whole weekend reading those letters and picked the best one. She lived in Arkansas and I sent her the bus fare. She stayed three days and went back to Arkansas. I never knew what went wrong.

I picked another letter and hired Margaret. She was a middle-aged woman who seemed efficient and was quite unattractive. This becomes important for the father of "two motherless children." I didn't know anything about Margaret, but she had a bunch of white uniforms and that made her look official. When I came home on Friday nights, it looked like Margaret had things under control.

After Margaret had been there three or four weeks, one rainy Sunday morning I took Roger to Sunday School and left Harriett at home with Margaret. When Roger and I returned, Margaret and Harriett were gone. I couldn't imagine where she had gone with Harriett in the pouring rain. I was frantic. I called the neighbors, who had seen nothing. I searched the house. Then I called the police.

I described Margaret and Harriett for the police, but I was unable to tell them how they left there. The police seemed amazed by the whole affair, but they said, "Keep cool, we will find them." I called my mother and father to let them share the worry. Soon, it was time for visiting hours at the hospital and Thorne would be expecting me. I couldn't go and tell her I had lost Harriett. I decided I had to tell her something. I sent my dad to tell her.

About five o'clock that evening, the police found Margaret and Harriett. They were in a large church in Independence. They evidently had spent the whole day in one church after another. They were traveling by bus. The police brought Harriett back. I never saw Margaret again.

In spite of the difficulties at home, I tried to keep Thorne's spirits up. While traveling I would write her about the business, my daily activities, and my love for her:

"When it rained last night, I thought of how you sometimes feel blue when it rains. I would like to teach you to like the windy rainy nights. It always reminds me of the sea and how high the waves are, and how the rain feels on my face on the bridge of a little ship. I can remember thinking, 'Dear God, don't forget these are men with souls on these little ships that are being tossed about.' On nights like that, as I peered through the storm, I would clench the rail with my hands and exhilaration would just run through me, and I would feel like laughing at the storm and yelling at it, 'Try and get me—just try.'

"I love you, dear, and I wouldn't try to fool you. If I ever found out any bad news about your condition, I would tell you. I couldn't do otherwise. I have always told you everything. When I say that Dr. Mantz says you are getting along fine, that is just what he says, and I try to read the inflection in every word. I am absolutely confident that you will get completely well. In the meantime, I will keep everything under control so you will not miss anything while you are resting."

None of the housekeepers stayed very long. When one left, I would take the next letter out of the basket and send for her. In between housekeepers, my folks would fill in. I left those children with whoever I could because I had to keep my job. I felt that I was just barely keeping it.

One night in between housekeepers, I was home alone. I had put Roger and Harriett in bed, and I was sitting there exhausted feeling very low. The doorbell rang and there was the preacher of our church, Reverend J. Lofton Hudsun. He didn't really know me. He had only come to the Wornall Road church about the time Thorne had gotten sick. However, I had gone to this church all my life and it was only natural that people would have told him about me and our desperate situation.

I hung up his hat and coat and we sat down. He said he had been wanting to talk to me. He said, "We need more young people in the church. You have an attractive younger brother who is single. If he and his friends would come to church, it would be easier to get the girls to come. Would you help get George to come to church?"

Yes, I said I would help him. Was there anything else? No, that was all. I got his hat and his coat. I shook hands with him at the door. He left and I never went back to the Wornall Road Baptist Church.

Dr. Keeler examined Thorne and looked over the facilities at the sanitarium. He picked out a room that had been part of the commissary where he could deliver the baby. He said we couldn't leave the delivery date up to Mother Nature because everything had to be exactly right. Delivering a baby in a hospital with what was considered a contagious disease was a delicate matter.

I tried to keep my spirits up and those of Thorne's as well, but I was always honest with her. In one letter, I wrote:

"When you get to the point that your wife is in a tuberculosis hospital and she is in a motherly way with your third child…

…and your other two children are making daily visits to the doctor escorted by your mother who is diametrically opposed to the doctor…

…and the housekeeper, to whom you have painted a pleasant picture of the quiet bliss of living in your home and caring for your children, is rapidly learning that she has attached herself to an American tragedy…

…there is just one thing to do.

"I considered lewd women, alcohol, and my work. After careful consideration, I decided on my work… We are having a contest at the Ford Motor Company called the 'Go Getter' contest, and it would be a great honor to win it. It would especially be an honor for me to win it, as no one, including me, ever suspects that I have a chance.

"When I get home this Friday night, the visits to the doctor will be over, and my kids will be as sound as a dollar. I will call Dr. Mantz, and he will say he has seen the x-ray, and my wife is improving rapidly, and there is nothing to worry about. My housekeeper, who I talked to on the phone a short while ago, will sound very content with her job as if she were enjoying it. So I will probably lapse back into a lethargic male who has nothing particular to do but kill time til his loving wife returns to his bed and board."

CHAPTER 7
AT HOME IN THE '50s

Love and Support

February 7, 1950, I wrote to Thorne:

"I stayed at the office all day. Then I got in the car and drove to Wichita. I just checked in the hotel and read your letter. I know you love me. I know you think of me. I know you send me messages. I am like a radio-controlled rocket. The days you feel bad and are blue, I have no ambition to work, and my talk is like dust on my tongue. The days that you feel good and cheer me on, I have a clean peppermint smile, and I enjoy the challenge of my work. But, I still like to hear what you are thinking. It is good for you to write it down sometimes, I think.

"Last week I told Bob White to tell the new manager that I would travel another sixty days. Today Simmons called me in and said I didn't need to think about looking for another job elsewhere. He said they would always need me whether

I could travel or not. He said if necessary they would make a zone close enough to Kansas City so I could come home every night. I told him I would like to start coming home every night by the first of April. The mood I was in, I wouldn't have been satisfied no matter what he said. But it does relieve my mind a little. It is a compromise, but it is an improvement."

In March, I continued my weekly letters from out of town. Among my many thoughts, I described to her my return home on Friday night:

"Driving five hours straight to get there. Dead tired, my back aches, need a bath. I'm hungry, but I don't want anything to eat. The kids are yelling and screaming and showing how spoiled they are. Won't eat their dinners—won't mind—whine, whine— they're getting worse—won't go to bed. I go out and listen to people talk about things I'm not interested in. I go home to bed disgusted. Take off my clothes, throw them on the floor—who cares? I'm about to get into bed. What's this? Looks like somebody in my bed! Somebody real small. I pull back the covers. It's Casey, sound asleep. I pick him up and he opens his eyes just a crack. 'I waited for you to come home, Daddy.' All of a sudden everything is very much worthwhile. How I love that boy! I'd like to hold him all night, but I put him in his bed and climb into mine. And ask God to make a better man out of me. God takes care of everything. I been trying to tell you, kid. After the dust comes the snow, and then the spring.

"I can't help but compare it to the war. The first six months in the Pacific seemed like six years. Then the fighting started. Time passes quick when you are fighting. Then the long journey home. When you get home you know it was worthwhile.

You've got something no one else has got. You've got that feeling, It's a wonderful world. It's wonderful to be alive. It's wonderful to love and be loved."

I tried to reassure her that my travels and her hospitalization were not going to have after- effects.

"I got your letter tonight. I was happy to get it. But I hasten to reassure you. You and I are not growing apart. You and I are partners in a great struggle. Most people are born, live, die and never know what a great struggle is. Just as comrades in battle form friendships that are deeper and more lasting than any they have ever known, you and I have formed a bond. We are absolutely necessary to each other. You are locked in my heart, and my heart would have to be cut out of my body before you could be taken away from me.

"When I see the sun on the green fields, I see it for both of us. When I take a deep breath of fresh spring air, I do it for the both of us."

"You are like a man who is serving a prison sentence from a crime for which he is innocent. Your sentence is tougher than his, because you are not allowed to wear yourself out on a rock pile. You are not allowed to be bitter and cynical against the society that sentenced wrongfully. You have no one or any group that you can hate. You can't cry out in anguish. You can't even ask anybody, 'Why have I been sentenced?' It's tough, awfully tough, and I know it. Believe me, my dear, you don't have to cry out loudly. I hear your cries."

"You have done a wonderful job of fighting your end of the battle. I am very proud of you. The reason that you have done so well, and the reason you will continue to win the game, no matter how many cards are stacked against you, is that you have confidence that God and your husband will not let you down. You know there is a wonderful life waiting for you when you recover. It is a life of love and a life of service. We desperately need you, but we can make it until you return to your rightful place. Even while you are there, the warmth of your love is felt in this house every day. I hope that by the same token, my confidence is felt in that hospital room every day."

"I think the toughest part of our hitch is behind us. The long months of preparation and training are behind us, and now we're sailing for Iwo Jima. Once the fighting starts, time passes quickly. Before you know it, we will be bellying up to the bar in Frisco saying, 'Make way for the boys who were there.'

I hired Mrs. Parker, a practical nurse, who had helped when Harriett was a baby. On the day our third child was born, May 18, 1950, Mrs. Parker and Thorne's parents waited outside in the car. Dr. Keeler said, "When the baby is born, I will lay him on that counter. You look at your watch. When he is forty-five minutes old, you pick him up and walk out of here. Don't let anybody touch him until you get him out of this building." When Charlie was forty-five minutes old, I picked him up and walked out to the car where JS, Kippie and Mrs. Parker were waiting. In a few minutes we were at home.

Mrs. Parker's job was to take care of the baby. I hired a large colored woman named Nora as housekeeper. Nora's job was to take care of Roger and Harriett and me. Harriett was going on two and Roger was going on four. Nora was big and strong and the children loved her. JS and Kippie went home and I went back to work. I felt like I really had to keep my job now.

The pressure in my job was terrific, but I had other pressures. I couldn't afford to miss a visiting period in the hospital as Thorne was isolated from the rest of the family. Children were not allowed in that building and Thorne had not held or even seen her baby. The doctor kept saying it is too soon to tell what effect the birth of the baby had had on her tuberculosis. Everyone said tuberculosis was highly contagious. My brother and I got x-rays regularly to see if we had gotten the disease.

When Charlie was two months old, Mrs. Parker left us and Nora took over the job of taking care of Charlie along with Harriett and Roger and me. I now had a baby boy a month old, a little girl not yet two and a boy a little over three. I felt that I needed my job more than ever, and that was becoming a problem. We had a new assistant manager named Ozzie Simmons. Ozzie was climbing the executive ladder and making a name for himself but he and I didn't see eye to eye.

It broke my heart when Nora told me she had to quit. I reached in the old basket and called Mrs. Hopkins. Mrs. Hopkins was a fifty-year-old woman from Arkansas who had raised nine children of her own. She was still available and would catch a bus and come to Kansas City as soon as I sent her the bus fare. Mrs. Hopkins turned out to be just what we needed. She was a large strong woman, and held Charlie in one arm in a very casual manner. She gave him a bottle of water before he had his bottle of milk. She said that made the milk and formula weaker and there was less chance of getting the colic. Something worked. He was a fat happy baby.

Mrs. Hopkins was still there when Christmas of 1950 arrived. The doctors let Thorne come home for two days. We didn't have a bedroom on the first floor so we rigged up a bed in the dining room with a partition around it. Thorne was definitely getting better. They had collapsed her left lung with air pressure to let it rest. They did this by pumping air into the lung cavity on the outside of the lung. I did my best to make her feel at home, but she had been gone almost sixteen months from Roger and Harriett and you can't re-establish that relationship in two days when one party is lying in bed. Baby Charlie was seven months old, and he had never seen her before. Mrs. Hopkins acted like she didn't want Thorne to hold the baby, and Thorne acted like she didn't want to anyway. I could tell that Thorne didn't like Mrs. Hopkins and Mrs. Hopkins acted like she didn't care.

When I took Thorne back to Leeds Sanitarium after two days at home, I realized that when she came home for good there would be a big adjustment for everybody. Thorne came home for good on the fifteenth of March, 1951. She had been in the hospital eighteen months. Most of that time she had been flat on her back. Her baby was ten months old and she still wasn't able to take care of him. In the two and a half months since Christmas, Mrs. Hopkins had quit and I had hired another housekeeper.

Hawley Motors

Early in March in 1951, I was on my way down to the family cabin on the Lake of the Ozarks to spend the weekend. I passed through the little town of Warsaw, Missouri, on my way down. Mr. Schroeder, the Ford dealer, who I had called on several times, had recently died and I stopped in to see what they were going to do with the Ford dealership. They had no sales staff but there was a bookkeeper, a parts manager and four mechanics working there. I learned they were asking thirty thousand dollars for the parts inventory, the tools, and equipment that went with the shop including the wrecker. This, of course, did not include the building which could be rented from the widow at a reasonable figure.

I walked down the street and looked at Warsaw. Warsaw is a county seat town on the Osage River, at the headwaters of the Lake of the Ozarks. The sign on the edge of town said population 952. As I looked at the scene down Main Street, I thought, "This town is fifty years behind the world that I am used too. It looks like Hannibal, Missouri,. when Tom Sawyer and Huck Finn lived there. My kids would love it, and I would be here to take care of them. I would not only be home every night, I would go home for lunch. If our housekeeper wouldn't come with us, we could hire one here who could live at home and walk to work."

I signed a contract contingent on my being able to borrow the money and get the Ford franchise.

I went to my boss at the Ford Motor Company on Monday and told him I was going to quit my job and buy the Ford dealership in Warsaw. He told me I had lost my mind.

I talked to my dad about quitting my job and buying the Ford dealership in Warsaw, and he was all for it. He said, "You know you can't travel any more when Thorne comes home. You will be close to our house on the Lake. I will even loan you money."

I decided that beside the thirty-thousand dollars I would need another ten thousand plus the equity in our house. I decided to borrow five thousand from my dad and five thousand from Thorne's dad. Then I would borrow twenty thousand from some lending institution. I went to Commercial Credit who had an office at Thirty-Third and Broadway in Kansas City, where people made payments on automobiles, washing machines, furniture, etc. One of the credit officers agreed to the loan because he knew me. He told his co-worker, "David Hawley used to run our parking lot at Muehlebach Field. He did a better job of accounting for the quarters than any of the young fellows we hired. I would bet on him."

Thorne had been home from the TB sanitarium less than a month when I received the money from Commercial Credit and paid Mrs. Schroeder for the Ford Dealership. I put my ten thousand dollars in the Community Bank and walked up the street and told my six employees that I was taking over. They seemed pleased as punch. We talked about who would unlock the building each morning and that we would open each morning about seven a.m. We were ready for business.

I had left Thorne in Kansas City to sell our house. I spent the first night in the Osage Hotel on the main street. By the time I was shaved and had eaten my breakfast and walked up to the Ford garage, it was a quarter of nine. Everyone there laughed at me when I walked in. Joan, the bookkeeper, said, "The first thing you have to learn is to get up in the morning." Then she offered to let me stay at her house until I found a place to live in Warsaw.

At the end of the first day, as the mechanics put their tools away and washed their hands, I could tell they were going somewhere together. I asked them where they were going. Wayne said they were going down to "CI's" to have a beer. I said, "Good, I will go with you." As the five of us started out the door, Joan said, "Where do you think you are going?" I said, "We are going down to CI's to have a beer." She said, "They are, but you aren't. You can't be the Ford dealer in Warsaw and drink beer in the public tavern. We'd lose half of our customers." I decided I had better take Joan's word for it for now. The mechanics went without me.

Joan's husband, Avis, was the barber with his father, Bill, in the barbershop right across the street from the garage. They lived on a farm about five miles south of Warsaw where they raised cattle. Avis was tall, handsome, friendly, a hard working young man. When they invited me to stay with them, I expected to share his chores on the farm. I didn't know he got up at four- thirty in the morning.

On my second day, a man came in and asked to meet the new Ford dealer. He was introduced as Brother Millfeldt. I recognized him at once: he had been in my English class at William Jewell. He told me he was the pastor of the Baptist church in Warsaw. He knew I was a Baptist. Tonight was Wednesday, church dinner night, and a good time for me to get acquainted. I went to the potluck and made many new friends.

We had an open house at the Ford dealership. The Ford Motor Company sent us three new cars and we offered free Cokes, cookies and door prizes. There was an article on the front page of the Benton County *Enterprise* with my picture. I smiled and introduced myself to everybody that came through the front door. Since it was Saturday, we had a lot of farmers and their wives and children. I didn't sell any new cars the day of our open house, but I had several people that sounded like they would be back.

I sold my first new car to Frank Brady, the prosecuting attorney and the senior lawyer of the county. My employees encouraged me to make a deal with him. He traded in his 1948 Ford and bought a new '51 model. But my employees weren't happy with me.

"You traded too fast. Mr. Brady would have given you more money. If you trade too fast, the buyer feels like he offered too much money." Everybody critiqued my sale. They suggested I kick a little gravel, look at the ground and do some thinking before making an offer.

The next day, a man from Climax Springs came in and wanted to buy Mr. Brady's '48 Ford. I told him what I wanted for it and he made me a lesser offer. I negotiated with him and sold the car. When I went out in the shop for my critique, I could see I hadn't pleased everyone. I still had a lot to learn.

I was still living with Joan and Avis on their farm. Thorne called and said she thought she had the house in Kansas City sold. I better find a place for my family to live in Warsaw. John Reser, the undertaker, offered to drive me around to see what was available.

Most of the homes were too small for our family. Mr. Reser showed me two larger homes that might be on the market eventually, but that current residents were elderly women in poor health.

We drove to another large house. "The old lady that lives here is just barely hanging on to life. But, she has been hanging on for over a year. I was sure we would have her service six months ago," Mr. Reser told me.

I was beginning to understand how frustrating the undertaking business could be.

We then drove to a nice-looking bungalow that was a block from the garage. "The lady that owns this house wants to rent it. It only has two bedrooms, but it has a finished second floor. The only trouble with it is it has no windows upstairs. She wants fifty dollars a month rent. If you told her you would pay her sixty a month if she would put a window in that room on the second floor, I think she would do it. Then, you could wait until one these other houses I have shown you becomes available." I signed a six-month lease.

Thorne and her real estate agent sold our house in Kansas City for two thousand dollars more than I expected. I got the rental house ready, and we moved in.

Thorne had left the Sanitarium with one lung collapsed so it could rest. To keep it that way, she needed air inserted in the cavity outside of her lung once a week. I wrote the State Medical Association and told them we were in Warsaw and needed the name of a good lung doctor nearby. They wrote back and said we were in luck. One of the best lung doctors in the state was located in nearby in Sedalia. We met Dr. Rhodes. This started a weekly pilgrimage to Sedalia to see Dr. Rhodes.

Thorne and I had mutually agreed that it was unnecessary to tell our new friends in Warsaw that she had recently been released from the tuberculosis sanitarium, that she was a Vassar graduate or that she was a Christian Scientist. We weren't ashamed of any of those things, but we didn't think they were the type of background our new friends would feel warm with.

I took Thorne to meet Brother Millfeldt at the Baptist Church. She got excited when she learned the church had a new organ. As a music major, Thorne had taken a course in playing the organ at college. She volunteered to play the new organ, and began directing the choir. She even had me sing tenor in the choir. I couldn't read music and had to memorize the part.

While we kept Thorne's Vassar connection to ourselves, we bragged about my graduating from William Jewell. In a Missouri county full of Baptists there is no better recommendation. When Brother Woolery was called to be our new preacher after Brother Millfeldt left, Thorne was his first convert. She joined the church and was baptized before a full house. Since I was a long time Baptist, I had my membership letter moved to the Warsaw church. The church had a lot of activities and we went to them all.

I joined the Bridge Club. I joined the Lions Club: it was the only service club in town and most of the merchants attended their weekly luncheon. Thorne joined the Book Club and we attended the Book Club's annual picnic.

I was going to work at seven-thirty a.m. and working until five-thirty at night. I worked all day Saturday, every Saturday. My mother, my dad and brother George would come through Friday night on their way to the cabin at the Lake, but I couldn't join them until Saturday night. Saturday was our biggest day for selling cars.

One afternoon I traded pickups with a farmer named Red Byrum. My pickup was not new but it was newer and in much better shape than the one he was trading in. We spent two hours negotiating. He finally said that was all the money he had. I said it wasn't enough. What else did he have, I asked. He thought a minute and said he had a new litter of seven pigs which he would throw in. I said, "Good, when will you bring them in?" He said he would bring them over to my house. We went to church supper that night and when we came home, in front of my house was the old pick-up with the seven little pigs in the backend. Roger and Harriett were thrilled. I built a pen for the pigs in the back yard but the pigs kept getting out the pen and were often seen running up the street into town. I sold five of the pigs at auction; the other two went to the neighbors to live until butchering time.

One of the regular customers in the garage was an elderly gentleman named Jim Atkins, who was a rural mail carrier. Jim owned a big house in Warsaw and wanted to move to his farm. He asked me to look at his house with the thought of buying it. Thorne and I walked through it. It was a big, old, well-built house that hadn't had any maintenance or modernization in a long time. It was in a good location in town on three acres of ground. I was very busy and didn't have time to think about buying a house.

Three days later, I was sitting at my desk with a customer when Jim Atkins stuck his head in the door and said, "Did you like my house?"

"Sure. It's a nice house." I said.

"Good. You just bought it." With that, he shut the door and left. When I went home for lunch, Thorne said that Mrs. Atkins had called and wanted to know how soon we were moving in.

That afternoon when I saw Jim walking down Main Street, I stopped my car and caught up with him. "If I bought your house, I would like to know what I paid for it." He stopped walking and looked at me for a minute as if I had asked him a silly question. "I wouldn't charge you any more than it is worth."

"I understand that. But, what is it worth?"

"Seventy-five hundred dollars," he said. This was a whole lot less than I had expected.

"I am not in any hurry for the money," he said. You will pay me someday. The only thing I am in a hurry to do is move out to my farm and I don't want to leave my house empty."

Frank Brady drew up a sales contract and I went to Kansas City and borrowed the money on an FHA loan for four-and-a-half percent.

When we moved into our new house, Jim Atkins left me two peacocks as a going away present. They were beautiful when they opened their tail feathers. The next morning, I found the two of them standing on my demonstrator car. There was bird dung completely covering the hood and most of top. I called Jim Atkins and gave the peacocks back. I washed off the car before it ruined the paint.

A farmer traded a horse named Sugar in on a used pick-up. Sugar was very gentle and I now had a place to keep her. Roger and Harriett rode Sugar around our new pasture. I bought them a sack of Omaline horse feed to feed her. I hadn't realized she was starving when we got her. The more she ate, the peppier she got. Pretty soon none of us could ride her. When a man offered me a fifty-dollar profit, I sold her.

We had Sugar long enough to realize how much fun a horse could be. When Avis Burton came across the street and said there was a man in the barbershop who wanted to sell a Shetland pony for fifty dollars, I bought it, sight unseen. Peanuts was ideal for our kids at that time. She was pretty and patient and slow. I bought a kids' saddle at the Sale Barn for twenty-five dollars and Roger and Harriett got to be good friends with Peanuts.

On one of Thorne's weekly visits to Sedalia, Dr. Rhodes x-rayed Thorne's chest and said there was no further need to keep her lung collapsed. He gave her a clean bill of health and told her to live a normal life. We were overjoyed.

Esther Bibb heard me say that I liked to read and she got me appointed to the Library Board. At the first meeting, I learned that there were some new books available free from the State Library, but there wasn't any place to put them. The Warsaw City Library was one room in the upstairs of the Community Building. There were three rows of free-standing bookcases full of books. I looked at the books and said, "Where in the world did these books come from?" I learned that when someone in Warsaw dies of old age, the books that weren't wanted by the family were given to the Warsaw library.

Over a period of years, the Warsaw library had accumulated the largest collection of *unreadable* books I had ever seen.

I suggested to the Board that we go through the books and pull out the ones that we felt sure would never be read, take them out back and burn them. This would make room for the new books. The Board said that whoever participated in the burning of the books would probably be tarred and feathered if they were lucky. And, as Esther Bibb said, "The people who dipped you in the hot tar would probably be people who couldn't even read."

The problem was, how to get rid of all those unreadable books without getting ourselves in hot water. After several suggestions, we decided to box them up and ship them to the State Penitentiary at Jefferson City. I said, "Those men have sinned against society and they deserve these books." This was my first civic job in Warsaw.

In 1951, the year that we moved to Warsaw, a group of Texans bought farms outside of Warsaw. There had been a drought in Texas for several years and I guess anything looked better than where they came from. These Texans added a lot of local color to the town.

We started a social club and wanted to hold dances in the old ice house. We decided to call our new club the Warsaw Literary and Athletic Society. At the first dance, one of the Texans roasted a goat, the ladies brought food and we had recorded music. It was a tremendous success.

Next, Thorne and I joined the Square Dance Club. We took lessons and got good at it. The other small towns in the area had square dance clubs which hosted fiestas and judges would award prizes. I never got to represent Warsaw in a contest, but Thorne did; she and her partner won.

Horse Tales

A gambler from Kansas City came in my garage one Saturday morning and said he wanted to sell a horse, cheap. The horse, according to him, was a young, small stallion half broke. The gambler, who was obviously down on his luck, said he would take fifty dollars for the horse. I bought him. Roger, who was eight, was ready for something more exciting than our Shetland pony, Peanuts.

That afternoon, I got a saddle and bridle and loaded the whole family in our station wagon to go out and meet our new horse, who Roger named "Crackerjack." The horse seemed very friendly. I put the bridle on him and he didn't object a bit. I led him around the pasture by the bridle and he followed perfectly. Eventually, we got a saddle on him, had Roger sit quietly on the horse, and felt confident that all was going well. I stepped back and Crackerjack immediately bucked Roger over his head on to the grass. Crackerjack just stood there. Roger was pleased with his performance. "Did you see that? I almost made it. I want to try it one more time."

It happened again…and again. I put Roger on a third time. This time, Roger stayed on through three of Crackerjack's bucks; then the little horse started to run. There was one tree in the pasture, it was a large Oak tree with a lower limb about as big as my leg. When Crackerjack ran under that tree, and Roger's head hit the limb, I thought it sounded like someone dropped a pumpkin on the sidewalk. We ran to where Roger was lying in the grass. His right arm and leg were under him at odd angles, and he looked very frightened.

"Are you all right?"

"I think my leg is broken."

"What about your arm?"

"I think that's broken too."

Can you move your head."

"I think my neck might be broken."

I happened to have twelve-inch planks in the station wagon. I drove the car in the pasture and Thorne and I lifted Roger into the backend by using the planks. We drove Roger to Dr. Salley's office. Dr. Salley was the local osteopath who boasted that he had delivered more babies in his dining room than the population of Warsaw. Since I was afraid to move him, Dr. Salley came out and examined Roger in the backend of the station wagon. When he finished examining him he said, "If that had been you on Crackerjack, all those things probably would be broken, but an eight-year-old boy's bones are a lot more rubbery and I don't think Roger has broken anything. However, he is going to be mighty sore for awhile."

The next day, I went back and using the bridle walked Crackerjack into town and into the pasture behind our house. He followed me like the family dog. He couldn't have been more cooperative. I got on him and he was peaceful. I sat there just a minute then his head went down, his hind-end went up into the air and I went over his head in a summersault and landed on the ground.

Later, when I described the experience to my employees, I had several volunteers to help with the horse. Most had spent their youth on a farm. One by one, they got on the calm, cooperative horse and were thrown. I announced that this concluded the first meeting of the Crackerjack Duster Club. Crackerjack acted like he was sorry everybody was leaving.

Our new friends, Texas cowboy John Gledhill and his beautiful wife, Betts, were at our house at a party. John wanted to see the horse. When John mounted Crackerjack, the horse stood perfectly still until John, too, ended up in the grass.

One afternoon in August, I came home early from the garage. I was feeling good and Crackerjack looked so friendly smiling at me over the back fence that I decided to give him one more chance. Thorne came out and watched. Same old story. The second time he bucked me over his head, I landed on my head and cut my forehead. Thorne said, "I wouldn't try that again if I were you."

I knew the rodeo was playing in Camdenton that week, about fifty miles from Warsaw. I gathered up Thorne and the kids and headed for Camdenton. We got to the rodeo a little bit early. I put Thorne and the kids in the best seats I could buy and I went looking for the cowboys that ride the bucking broncos. I found just what I was looking for. I told this young cowboy that I had a little horse I couldn't stay on, and I offered to pay him to give me a lesson. He said it sounded to him like I was sitting straight up in the saddle and not leaning back far enough. He said, "You watch me in the show tonight, and if you still want a lesson, come look me up after the show." I watched him and the other riders in the rodeo and I could see that he was right. I could hardly wait to get home and try it.

The next morning when Crackerjack gave me that knowing smile, I said, "Have I got a surprise for you." Well, it was exciting and the outcome was in doubt, but I stayed on. After a half dozen bucks and I was still there, Crackerjack trotted around the pasture with me on his back and my whole family cheered. I rode him every day for the next five days, and by then the kids wanted to ride him. Two weeks after we had all ridden him and I thought he was perfectly safe, he unexpectedly bucked Harriett off and put a big knot on her head. I decided he was more dangerous than ever and I would get rid of him. We already had another horse, Babe, who was Thorne's horse. We didn't need Crackerjack.

I loaded Crackerjack in a used truck with side racks that the garage owned and drove him down to call on a horse trader named Lawrence Arnold. I told him I didn't think the horse was right for our little girl to ride. He praised the appearance of Crackerjack and said he would like to have him. He also said he had a very nice mare named Jenny that would make a nice family horse. I rode her and liked her. After digging holes in the gravel and spitting a lot, I agreed to give twenty-five dollars and my valuable horse, Crackerjack, for his horse, Jenny. He agreed, and we loaded Jenny in my truck.

I tried riding Jenny at home but she kept raring up and I would slide over her back. I told John Gledhill I had a new horse and a new problem. He laughed and said that was an old problem and easily handled. He said, "You cut yourself a club about two feet long and when she starts up, you hit her over the head right between the ears. She will put her feet right back on the ground." I said it was wonderful to have a real cowboy for a friend and would he like to hit Jenny over the head for me. He said sure, he would do that for me.

We met the next afternoon and I rode Babe and John rode Jenny. We rode out to the same field where I had had the trouble the day before. When we got to the end of the field, I gave the signal and went to the left on Babe and John turned right on Jenny. I heard the "clonk" when John hit Jenny on the head, and I turned in time to see the horse fall over backwards with John still in the saddle. For a moment, they were both on the ground with John on the bottom. Then the horse scrambled up on her feet and John lay on the ground. I jumped off Babe and stood over him. He was grimacing but still grinning. "I am not going to ride any more of your horses. They are too dangerous." We needed to find a new home for Jenny.

On my way home from my dad's house on the lake one Sunday evening, I passed a farm where a man was riding a horse. I recognized the man. It was Sam Croy, one of the displaced Texans who had moved to Warsaw. I liked the looks of the horse he was riding, and I stopped to visit with him. When I admired his horse, he insisted that I ride him and see what a nice gait he had. I rode him, and if it is possible to fall in love with a horse, I fell for Brownie.

The following week, Sam Croy came into Warsaw to trade trucks. While we were digging holes in the gravel with our shoe tips and spitting into them, I asked him if he would do me a big favor and look at a mare that I owned and tell me if he thought she was going to have a colt. I thought she was getting fatter than she should, and I had begun to wonder if she was in foal.

I got a piece of string and we measured around Jenny's stomach in several places. After measuring her, Sam said, "Yes, I definitely think she is going to have a colt."

I talked him into buying the truck, and trading horses with me. He could have Jenny and the colt, and I would take Brownie.

That night I was jubilant as I rode Brownie around our pasture. He was the first good horse I had ever owned. I was now ready to join the riding club. This horse could rack, which is a very comfortable gait with which I could cover a lot of ground. We bought a buggy with side curtains and a harness. Everybody wanted to borrow my buggy. I couldn't resist loaning it to Dr. Rhodes when he said he wanted to make a few house calls.

On a trip to Kansas City, I saw the movie *Ben Hur*. I loved it and came home and had my body shop build me a chariot out of an oil drum and some bicycle wheels. I had the harness and I had the horse. Behind the stores on Main Street there was a piece of flat land where the river overflowed every year. When it was dry, which it was in the summer, it was an ideal place for a chariot race. I had gone horse crazy. I even sent away to a mail order house and got a set of rubber horse shoes so Brownie wouldn't slip on the blacktop when he ran down Main Street.

The African Queen

We had a new Game Warden in our town named Duke Ponder. I got acquainted with him when he had his car worked on in the garage and we went on a canoe trip together. One day Duke Ponder came to see me and asked me if I wanted to buy a boat. He had found a steel boat in a dried-up slough on a backwater of the Lake that hadn't been used in years. The inboard engine had been ruined and all that was left was the steel hull. The Union Electric Company had agreed to sell it for one hundred dollars "as is" where it was sitting. Duke Ponder hadn't been able to move it and he reasoned that I could move it with the wrecker that belonged to the Ford Garage.

When we went out to get it with the wrecker and a borrowed trailer, Wilbur See said it looked just like the boat in the movie, *The African Queen*. From then on that boat was the African Queen. We brought the Queen into the Ford Garage where we proceeded with the overhaul and refitting. We built a wooden floor or main deck with benches along the sides. We built a ladder from the lower deck to the upper deck, and I bought a twenty-five horsepower used outboard motor for one hundred dollars. The upper deck was good for sunbathing, diving, moonlight riding, and it greatly increased the number of passengers I could carry.

The Lake of the Ozarks was a man-made lake that was formed by damming the Osage River. Acquiring the African Queen gave me an access to that Lake that was wonderful. It was inexpensive to own and operate and it was unhurtable. We had picnics every night. We would go up the river until we found a good place to swim. We would beach the African Queen, build a fire, cook our dinner, drink beer, sing songs, and have a moonlight cruise home. C I Searcy, the proprietor of the local saloon, told one of my mechanics one evening, "I think they are drinking more beer on the African Queen than they are in my saloon."

After we had lived in Warsaw one year, Dr. Rhodes announced that the x-rays showed Thorne's lung completely clear and there was no more problem with tuberculosis.

Thorne told me she was once again pregnant. The only M.D. in Warsaw at that time was a young clean-cut looking man named Dr. David Glenn. He was a good Bridge player, a good golfer, and had a pretty wife. He was also in big trouble with me. He drove a Ford and had recently come to the garage and asked me how much I would trade it for a new car. I made him what I thought was a very reasonable offer. He said he would think about it and he got in his car and drove to Windsor, Missouri. The dealer in Windsor sold him a car for twenty-five dollars less.

Not having any other options, I went to Dr. Glenn and told him Thorne was pregnant and did he want to deliver the baby. He said, "Yes."

I said, "Fine. Now here is what I want you to do. You figure out how much you will do it for including the prenatal visits and including the circumcision if it is a boy, the whole ball of wax. After you tell me, I am going to Sedalia and see if any doctor at the hospital will do it for any less. It doesn't make any difference to Thorne who delivers it. If I don't beat your price, I will tell you that you have the job." Dr. Glenn called me the next day and said he would do it for sixty dollars. I didn't bother going to Sedalia: our last baby had cost five hundred dollars and the one before that had cost three hundred. I decided at sixty dollars, Dr. Glenn was trying to make up for buying his car in Windsor.

Our son George was born that spring, in 1955.

I joined the Chamber of Commerce in Warsaw and was elected to be a member of the Warsaw School Board. The Warsaw School District had been reorganized some time before and all the one-room school houses in the district had been closed and the students were bussed into Warsaw. The school was a big business. We hired the teachers, and it wasn't always an easy job. We didn't pay as much money as the cities or the larger towns. One of our weak spots was a music teacher. The current music teacher when I went on the board couldn't keep order. The students threw their chairs out the window. Unfortunately, the room was on the second floor. This teacher quit in the middle of the semester.

One Saturday morning, I was standing out in front of the Ford dealership when a young man in his late twenties approached me and said, "I hear you need a music teacher in the high school." I acknowledged that we did, and he said, "Well, I can teach music, and I would like to talk to you about the job."

Bill Jessee had worked his way through college playing in a band but had no real teaching experience. He didn't much like kids. But we hired him. The amazing thing about him was that no matter how gruff he was, the kids liked him. Every kid in high school wanted to rent an instrument and play in Mr. Jessee's band.

When summer came, we hired Bill Jessee to organize and direct the City Band that played Saturday nights on the courthouse lawn. Some of the older citizens of the town joined the kids and played in his band. He didn't have any trouble getting all the musicians he wanted.

Community Activist

As time went by, I was getting better at trading cars. Experience can be an expensive teacher, especially in the car business. The residents of Warsaw and its trade area had been educating me. I had gotten a lot better at kicking the gravel and spitting in the hole. I had learned to not speak quickly but to remain quiet and eventually the other guy will commit himself. Sometimes, you have to wait quite a while. I was trading for many more things than cars. My customers wanted to trade in horses, pigs, cattle (including a Brahma bull) and boats on cars. There was a weekly livestock auction, and anything I traded for I sold at the auction.

I had discovered that although many of the people who lived in Warsaw loved to fish, very few of them could swim. When I went with the Scout troop, I had never seen so many boys that couldn't swim. They didn't have any place to learn. The town backed up to the Lake of the Ozarks, but no one swam in it at Warsaw. When I was approached to run for president of the Warsaw Chamber of Commerce, I said I would run and, if elected, the Chamber could help me build a municipal swimming pool. I was elected and with the Chamber's blessing started looking to see where the money would come from. I learned the City had no money and we would have to have a bond issue passed to raise the money. We formed a committee. We held meetings. We gave speeches and wrote articles for the paper. The bond issue passed. They built a very nice pool in the City Park. We needed a lifeguard that first summer that had a senior Red Cross life-saving certificate. Thorne took the course and got the certificate. She lifeguarded until we could get someone else. The kids in Warsaw learned to swim overnight.

Roger joined the Cub Scouts, and Thorne became a den mother. I was soon elected Treasurer of the pack. I soon realized it was an extremely hard job. There were twenty-seven boys in the den and they each paid dues of five cents a week. I collected this money and then I used it to pay for the badges and decorations on their uniforms that they earned every month. The boys were supposed to earn this money by doing constructive things. Consequently, half of them didn't have it on den meeting night. I figured we weren't quite breaking even. Sometimes the kids gave me a nickel and I put it in my pocket. Other times, I would pay the difference and not keep track of who paid and who didn't.

I didn't have any trouble until Roger graduated from Cub Scouts to Boy Scouts, and I gave up the job. The man who replaced me couldn't understand my system. He acted like he had discovered a teller at the bank that was putting the money in his pocket. I began to wonder if I had been making a profit out of the dues.

Sometimes, on a hot summer night, Thorne and I would sleep in a double bed on our front porch. One morning while we were sleeping there, we were awakened by our son, Charlie, who was running down the stairs screaming. He burst through the front door and ran to the side of the bed.

On his arm was one of those nasty brown creatures that has a tail that curves up over his back and forms a partial circle. Thorne sat up and brushed it off of Charlie's arm. Instead of being brushed off, it ran up Thorne's arm and bit her. It hurt like a wasp sting when it bit her. After we finally got the centipede killed, we wondered what to do. I had always heard they were deadly poisonous, but that is hard to believe when you wife has just been bitten by one, especially when she is a good Christian Scientist. I thought about calling Dr. Rhodes, but it was five-thirty in the morning. Thorne gave up sleeping and started fixing breakfast. We all got up and watched her. By seven o'clock, she had a welt on the inside of her lower arm that was a foot long and an inch high. I finally called Dr. Rhodes. I told him about the centipede.

"How long ago did it bite her, Dave?"

"It was about five-thirty; a little over two hours ago."

There was a pause while I waited for an answer. Finally, he said, "Did she die?"

"No."

"Well, that's great, Dave. I have always heard they were deadly poisonous, too. Now we know they aren't."

After I had been in Warsaw six years, I was asked to be the speaker at the annual Phi Gamma Delta Norris Pig Dinner at William Jewell College.

I told them about my college days, my early employment, my Navy experiences and what it was like to be a captain. Then I shared with them the joys of living in a small town:

"I believe there is a future for the young college graduate who bucks the population trend and makes his living in the small Missouri town.

First: You are closer to business opportunities that are of a size you can handle when they arise. You are on the spot when a business or property is ready to change hands. There are probably more opportunities in Kansas City, but you don't know about them.

Second: It is easier to borrow money because in a small town, banking has a tendency to be done on a personal basis.

My third reason is there is less competition. Most of the smart young men with your education have gone to the city to work. It is a pretty well-established fact that in order to be happy, a person has to be interested in some cause, somebody, something other than himself. In a man my age, it is a much healthier thing for him to be interested in the Boy Scouts than in his neighbor's wife. How much better if his outside interest is of a constructive nature! In a small town, a young eager man not only has a world of opportunity for service, he will be drafted into the job if he hesitates to say no. It's a lot of fun to be a big frog in a little puddle. If you work at it, you might even be invited to be the speaker at the annual Norris Pig Dinner at the Phi Gam House at William Jewell College, and no one could ask for a higher honor than that."

Camping

In 1958, I had lived in Warsaw seven years when my good friend, Bill Neff, suggested we take the two families and go to Colorado on a camping trip. We each had four kids, a station wagon, and a cooperative wife. We had been on a camping trip with them before when we went canoeing. The canoeing trip had been a lot of fun so I agreed to go to Colorado. We decided to go to Rocky Mountain National Park and camp out in a campground called Glacier Basin. Katie Neff was twelve years old, Roger Hawley was eleven, Billy Neff was ten, and Harriett Hawley was nine. Charlie Hawley was eight. Becky Neff and George Hawley were both three years old, and Debby Neff was two. Everybody was glad to get out of their car when we got to Glacier Basin. It was evening when we got there, and we could see it was beautiful at nine thousand feet. We put up our tents and built a fire. By the time we cooked and ate our supper, everyone was ready for bed. We blew up our air mattresses, put the sleeping bags on top of them, and went to sleep.

The next morning I discovered there was over an inch of cold water everywhere in the tent. All of our clothes and socks and shoes were floating in the water. It was five-thirty in the morning and pitch black outside. When I stepped in my bare feet out of the sleeping bag, I stood in an inch of ice cold water. I went out of the tent to escape from the water and found there was two inches of snow covering everything. We had set up our tents where the water ran to when the snow melted. Poor choice. Everyone was trying to find something dry to put on. Bill Neff built a fire, and that wasn't easy. We stood around the fire and tried to stay warm and wait for daylight. Bill made a big pot of oatmeal and everybody stood and ate it. When it began to get light we drove in to the Laundromat in Estes Park and dried our clothes. We didn't have a Laundromat in Warsaw in those days, and it seemed like a miracle. We went back to our campsite, moved our tents to high ground and started to explore the park. The sun came out and the snow was gone by noon. I loved the whole trip and I think everybody else did.

The second summer we went to Rocky Mountain National Park with the Neffs was even more successful than the first. We slept on the ground in our tent, but the Neffs had bought an old travel trailer that they towed behind their car and slept in. The air was great; the scenery was great; and we took some fun hikes. We could see Long's Peak from our tent, and I had wondered how big a deal it would be to climb it. A couple days later, when we were in the museum, I bought a book called How to Climb Long's Peak. The book started out with the history of Long's Peak, then explained how all kinds of people had climbed it. Old ladies had climbed it. A man with one leg had climbed it. Anyone who went to Colorado on vacation and didn't climb it had missed the high point of the trip. I told Bill Neff about it and tried to get him to read the book, but he wasn't too interested. He said he would go camping with us, but he wasn't too interested in climbing the mountain.

We drove out to Colorado in the third week in June. We planned to stay a week, and I planned to climb the mountain on the next-to last day. Bill Neff didn't want to go but he drove into town and bought a pair of hiking shoes so he could go. That evening, he called the ranger station to ask if they thought it was safe for us to take the boys who had never climbed anything. Bill reported back that the Ranger recommended that we "forget about it." I replied that the Ranger had probably not read the book.

The next morning when we got to where the trail up the mountain to Boulder Field began, there was a sign that said, "It is too early in the season to climb Long's Peak. There is still too much snow. Check with the Ranger station for possible times."

I said, "Don't worry. An old lady with one leg climbed this mountain."

We started up the path to the Boulder Field. The mountain was not completely covered with snow but every place that was flat had snow on it.

We began to hike to the summit, climbing over boulders and treacherous slopes. I referred again to the book. "These snow banks become very icy. On an average year they are risky for inexperienced climbers until July 20 or later. Ask the ranger before attempting the North Face until late July." We were climbing it in June and by now we all realized we had come a little early.

When we finally reached the top, we found a fairly flat surface as big as a football field, covered with rocks about the size of basketballs. In the middle there was a pile of rocks with a brass tube. The book said we should sign the register in the tube. When Charlie signed it, he proudly wrote that he was ten years old. The wind was blowing so hard that I had to lie down between the rocks to read the book. It was not a pleasant place to spend any time. Furthermore, we were two hours later than the book said you should depart from the top. Bill Neff was anxious to start down.

Bill Neff went first with Billy following him. Roger, Charlie and I took our time. When we got to the bottom, Thorne was waiting in our car, but no sign of the Neffs. Thorne said Helen had been waiting and taken them back to camp.

Thorne and Helen had prepared a big chicken dinner and although we were very tired, we all enjoyed it. All except Bill Neff. He never came out of his trailer. Immediately after supper, we went to bed and to sleep. I was awakened at five-thirty in the morning by the sound of a car that sounded very close to the tent. I stuck my head out of the tent just in time to see the Neffs' car leaving the campground pulling their trailer. I couldn't believe they would leave without saying "goodbye." When I thought a minute, I realized we had not spoken to each other since we left the top of Long's Peak. After breakfast, we leisurely took down out tent, packed the car and started for home.

Brownie & Chanticleer

I was keeping my horse, Brownie, in the three-acre field behind my house. I had a big sack of Omaline, which is an expensive horse feed, in the back end of an old Plymouth station wagon in my garage. Every morning while Thorne was getting breakfast, I would fill a coffee can full of Omaline out of the Plymouth and take it out and put it in a bucket for my favorite horse, Brownie. Sometimes our rooster, Chanticleer, would eat it as well. The rooster would be waiting by the Plymouth hoping I would spill a little of the Omaline on the ground

One morning I was about to feed my horse when I got a telephone call from the garage, and they wanted me down there right away. Thorne had gone on an early morning grocery run in my car, so I got out the old Plymouth, which I had never used, and started for the garage. A block and a half from our house was a stop sign. When I stopped, I automatically looked out of the rearview mirror and was surprised to see Chanticleer running down the middle of the street behind the Plymouth. His neck was stretched out, his wings flapping and he was going for it. When he got up to the car, I opened the door on the passenger side and he jumped in. He stayed in the car eating Omaline while I did my business at the garage and then I took him home.

The next morning, instead of feeding my horse, I got in the Plymouth and drove off. When I got to the stop sign, I looked back and sure enough, here came the rooster on the run with his wings flapping. I rewarded him with Omaline and took him home. I realized I had a wonderful thing here.

I have a rooster that chases cars. I better keep this very quiet until all the bets are down. If I could get Chanticleer to chase my Plymouth down Main Street, I could win a lot of money and both would be famous.

CHAPTER 8
MOVING ON

Sex Education at Warsaw High

Warsaw High School did not have a football team, but we made up for it with our basketball team. The greatest recognition in our high school, and our community, went to the basketball players. The star of the basketball team this year was a boy named Henry and he went steady with a girl named Ruth. They were the unquestioned king and queen of the Senior class. One day, Henry and Ruth announced that the day before, they had driven to Sedalia and been married by the justice of the peace. The next day, everyone knew that Ruth was pregnant. They received the congratulations of their friends and several people gave showers for them. Many people said, "What a lovely young couple." Ruth told some of her close friends confidently that her pregnancy had not been an accident. She wanted to make sure of Henry before he went away to school and formed some other alliance. Six weeks later, one of Ruth's close friends announced she was pregnant and her steady boyfriend married her. Two weeks later, another of Ruth's close friends announced she was married. These girls were the leaders of the class and they were marrying the most eligible boys. Getting pregnant in our Senior class spread like the measles.

I was the president of the School Board, and all of a sudden it was the school's fault. One irate father who I knew well called me up and said we sure doing a hell of a poor job running that school. I told him I didn't have anything to do with his daughter getting pregnant and I personally doubted that it had occurred at school. The father said he had a good notion to come down and punch me in the nose. Brother Pope, the minister of the Christian Church, who I thought was a good friend of mine, told me I had really missed the boat. I asked him what I should have done. He said, "The very instant one of those girls got pregnant, you should have kicked them out of school." Meanwhile, the girls continued to get pregnant and many of the parents blamed it on the school.

We had a new young preacher at the Baptist Church where I was a member. He was the speaker at the school assembly one afternoon. In the middle of the speech, Mr. Freund called me at the Ford garage and said, "We are in big trouble. Your preacher is speaking to the student body, including the junior high, on the subject of sexuality. Those young kids' parents aren't going to like this."

I said, "If you wait till kids are fourteen to tell them about sex, in some cases I imagine you are too late."

Mr. Freund said, "I am just warning you to get ready. There is going to be a lot of criticism." He was right. I took the poor minister and his wife down to my dad's cabin on the lake. I left them there by themselves for a week until the worst blew over.

Thorne liked the minister and was mad at the church for being so hard on him. She announced she was through being a Baptist and was not going back there anymore. She said she did not believe the way the people in that church believed, and since it was their church, she didn't think she should try to change them. I could feel my foundation in Warsaw begin to totter. All the girls in the Senior class were on their way to getting pregnant, and my wife was going to leave the Baptist Church.

That weekend, down at my dad's cabin at the lake, my brother George said to me, "Why don't you sell your business in Warsaw and come to Kansas City and run the Shryock Realty Company. The guy who runs it now is going to be sixty-five in six months. He says that unless we sell him a big chunk of the stock at a very cheap price, he will retire. He is using this as a threat to scare us. It doesn't scare me because I think that anybody could do a better job of running the company than he is doing."

The Shryock Realty Co. was an old well-established real estate company that was started by the grandfather of George's wife Nancy. After Nancy's grandfather, Mr. Shryock, died in 1940, her father, Frank Wilkinson, ran the company until his death in 1958. The stock in the company belonged to Mrs. Wilkinson and her two daughters, but no member of the family worked at the Shryock Realty. It was now 1961 and according to my brother, who was one of the directors of the company, it hadn't done much but clip coupons for the last three years. I told him I wasn't interested. I did not tell Thorne about George's offer.

A few days later, Thorne said to me, "I think it is about time for us to move on from Warsaw. How unusual to live in a town where there is not one Negro or one Jew. No foreign language in taught in the high school. I think our children deserve a bigger window on the world than they are getting here."

I said, "What you really mean is that Harriett is thirteen and you are wondering if all the girls in her Senior class are going to be pregnant."

That weekend at the lake, George brought up Shryock Realty again. He said, "The Shryock Realty Company has more money than a small town bank. It should be making money but it isn't. You could understudy the present president for six months. Let him retire, and then you could run it. I am sure that anything you did would look good."

Changing Times

The U.S. engineers decided, after many years of politicking, to build a dam two miles out of Warsaw that would cost four hundred million dollars. It would prevent flooding on the Osage and the Missouri Rivers. It would also create a giant recreational facility right next to Warsaw. The people in our town and our county had been for or against this dam for many years and now it was going to happen. The U.S. Congress had authorized it. All the merchants in Warsaw felt that they were going to prosper with all this new business.

A couple days after my brother had mentioned the Shryock Realty Company for the second time and my wife had said that our children deserved a bigger window on the world, a man named Mr. Eaton walked into my office and said he would like to buy my business. I knew him. He had been a successful tractor dealer. He was the right age to please the Ford Motor Company and I was sure he could raise the money.

I said, "It just so happens that a couple days ago I was offered a good job in Kansas City. You give me fifteen minutes and I will tell you what I will take for this business and walk out the door. Then we will know if you are still interested and if we should talk."

It was lunch time and I was the only one in the office. In less than fifteen minutes, I figured what I thought would be the right price and when I told Mr. Eaton, he said that would be fine. He would take it. I said that before I would sell it to him, I wanted to give Darwin Schroeder, the parts man, the opportunity to buy it. Darwin's father had owned the business before I did. When Mr. Schroeder died and I bought it, Darwin was only nineteen years old. Now, he was twenty-nine and I felt I owed him the first refusal. If he turned it down, I would go to Kansas City and nail down my new job. Then the buyer and I would go to the Ford Motor Co. and ask for their blessing.

After Darwin and his wife and mother spent a sleepless night, he turned it down. My brother George held a meeting at Shryock Realty and said I could start anytime I wanted. The Ford Motor Company said I was selling the dealership too high, but maybe with the new dam coming on, it was justified. They approved Mr. Eaton, and Mr. Eaton gave me an earnest-money check. I told my employees and the news spread throughout the town.

The next day I received a telephone call from Mrs. Rhodes, the mother of the doctor. She said she had heard that I had sold my business. If this meant that I was leaving town, she would like to buy my house. I told her that no one was at home. The house was unlocked and she was welcome to browse through it. I also told her what I wanted for it. In a couple hours, Mrs. Rhodes came in the garage and handed me a check for one thousand dollars. She said, "I will give you the rest of the money whenever the papers are ready." When I bought that house from Jim Atkins, he had been trying to sell it for years. I raised the price considerably and sold it before I told anybody I wanted to.

That same day, I received a telephone call at the garage from a well-to-do older man who wanted to know what I was going to do with my horses. He said, "I want to buy the horse that your youngest boy rode in the Thanksgiving Day parade." That was Thorne's horse, Babe. In the next couple of days, I sold everything I owned but my wife and kids and the dog.

I was getting a haircut and listening to the loafers in the barbershop when the barber said, "What are you going to do with that old rooster up at your house? It's too old and tough to be good for anything. I'll give you five dollars for it to get it out of your way." One of the loafers spoke up: "Are you talking about the rooster that chases cars? He won't take five dollars for that one. It's worth a fortune." I left them talking about what should be done with Chanticleer. About an hour later, I had a call from Dr. Rhodes. He said, "I heard you were trying to sell my rooster at the barber shop. That rooster goes with the house." I agreed and said I would deed the rooster with the house.

That night at dinner, my children sounded like they didn't want to move back to Kansas City. I told them, "We are doing this for me." I said, "I am only forty-two years old, and I spend over half of my time playing cowboy, playing boat, canoeing, camping out, climbing mountains, to say nothing of playing golf and hunting ducks. I need a new challenge. I have an opportunity to run this company that has plenty of money. I can play at the big table. I am too young to retire. This is a new adventure for all of us. We are going to be free to make a lot of new choices. It will be a whole new world and we are going to

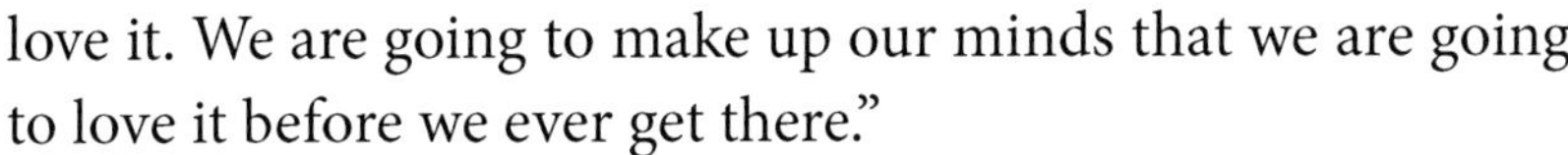

love it. We are going to make up our minds that we are going to love it before we ever get there."

AFTERWORD

The Hawleys did, in fact, move back to Kansas City and loved it. David went to work for Shryock Realty as their manager and had a successful career there.

Through the years, as the children matured, David continued to write letters, dispensing much advice and praise. He especially enjoyed the challenges of rearing his sons, and gave them the same latitude his own father had given him. He often told his children, "No matter what kind of trouble you get into, I'll be there with a net under the tightrope." He encouraged them to take risks, to see opportunities for learning, and mostly, to have fun. Amidst their active daily lives, there was music: the children recall lively evenings singing together at home. In time they left home, traveled the world, went off to college and started families of their own.

When not at work, David and Thorne traveled, entertained, and enjoyed weekends skiing, boating and playing tennis, always looking for another adventure.

On Mothers Day, 1979, youngest son George suffered massive head injury in a motorcycle accident. One week later, David retired from his job on his 60th birthday. David took George's accident to heart and, instead of sailing around the world with George as he had planned, spent much of his remaining years helping care for his son. David retained a positive attitude, kept in open communication with friends and family, and never lost his sense of humor.

In the late 1980s David suffered a heart attack and stroke. Being limited in speech was a real challenge for him, as he still had stories to tell. David Hawley died at home in 1995 at the age of 76.

Daughter Harriett recalled later of her dad, "He was the most upbeat person you will ever meet and he supported and entertained us always." Even today, his tales of a unique and adventurous life continue to entertain.